PET PROTECTION LEGAL CARE PLAN™

Financial and Legal Planning to Protect Your Companion Pet

Estate Planning Information for My Pet... *Just in Case*

- Describe Your Pet and Their Daily Schedule
- Identify the Pet Caregiver/Guardian, Pet Financial Caregiver/Trustee & Other Pet Care Advisors
- Locate Your Pet's Medical Information/History and Emergency Preparedness Plan
- Complete the "*Pet Protection Daily Care Guide*™" and the "*Pet Protection Trust*"
- Complete Your Pet's End-of-Life Plan and Care Instructions

MARY G. ANDERSON

with Francis Burton Doyle, Esq., Family Estate Planning Attorney

Notice to Readers

This book is intended to provide general educational information regarding the estate planning process required for pet owners to protect their companion pet. None of the information, advice, or suggestions in this publication is intended to take the place of an attorney, financial advisor, physician, veterinarian, therapist or professional in the relevant subject area. The information presented throughout this document should not be interpreted as a substitute for one's own responsible evaluation of information, products, or services.

Disclaimer

This publication is not a substitute for legal advice; it is designed to inform persons about estate planning for their companion animals/pets/service pets. Future changes in laws cannot be predicted and statements in this publication are based solely on the legal statutes in force on the date of publication. While every effort is made to provide the best, most accurate and most current information, guarantees cannot be made. If you have questions and/or concerns, please seek the counsel of an attorney, financial planner or other estate planning professional. This publication is for informational purposes only and is not intended and should not be construed as legal, medical or financial advice. This information is not intended to create, and receipt of it does not constitute, a lawyer-client relationship. Viewers should not act upon this information without seeking professional counsel as necessary. Nothing in this document should be considered personalized legal, medical, or financial advice.

The information contained in this guide has been obtained from sources believed to be reliable, but we cannot guarantee its accuracy or completeness. This educational material contains the opinions and ideas of the author and is designed to provide useful information in regard to its subject matter. The information is written in general terms and is not intended as a substitute for specific advice regarding individual investment, tax or legal planning. The authors, publisher and presenter specifically disclaim any responsibility for liability, loss or risk, personal or otherwise, that is incurred as a consequence, directly or indirectly, of the use and application of any of the contents of this information. You must consult with your legal, tax and medical professional advisors regarding your personal circumstances.

Terms of Use

You are given a one-time, non-transferable, "personal use" license to this product. You cannot distribute it or share it with other individuals. Also, there are no resale rights or private label rights granted when purchasing this document. In other words, it's for your own personal use only.

Copyright

All rights reserved. No part of this book may be reproduced or transmitted in any form or by any means, graphic, electronic, or mechanical, including photocopying, scanning, recording, taping or by any information storage retrieval system, without the written permission of the publisher except in the case of brief quotations embodied in critical articles and reviews.

ISBN 978-0-9863872-4-1
Published in the United States of America by *Yellow Brick Road Publishing* © 2015
For additional information, visit us online at www.petprotectionlegalcareplan.com.

"Men have forgotten this truth,"
said the fox, "but you must never forget it.
You become responsible, forever,
for what you have tamed...."
~Antoine de Saint-Exupery, *The Little Prince*

Both authors are dedicated to providing the guidance and resources to support individuals and families to create a "*Pet Protection Legal Care Plan*" for every companion pet in the U.S.! Our goal is to build relationships and referral networks with other estate planning attorneys, veterinarians, animal rescue organizations, pet boarding facilities, pet groomers, dog walkers, pet supply stores, etc., across the country to join us in promoting the concept of pet estate and end-of-life planning. Please contact us if you would like us to speak to your group about the importance of creating both an estate plan and a *Pet Protection Trust* to protect your loved ones *(and your furry friends)*. We are proud to donate 10% of our profits to provide pet trusts and pet protection planning services to our animal charity partners throughout the country. We can be reached at www.petprotectionlegalcareplan.com.

Dedication

"Thorns may hurt you, men desert you, sunlight turns to fog;
but you're never friendless ever, if you have a dog."
~Douglas Mallock

This book is dedicated to Zeus ...

To My Handsome Boy Zeus,
who brought so much energy and love to my life,
I miss you so much.
March 11, 2009 ~ January 10, 2012

Contents

Preface

Every day of my life, from dawn to dusk, the pets I have known and loved since childhood, have inspired me through the *'thick and thin'* of life's various trials and tribulations. This book was born from my deep love of animals and my belief that the companionship of a pet can help to heal a broken heart, soothe a sick child and lift the spirits of an elder. Our pets love us unconditionally and we need to protect their lives.

Whether you're away from your pet for a few days, a month or forever, you will know that he or she is being taken care of and living the life you would want for them because you have set up a *Pet Protection Trust*. I have worked closely with an experienced California-based *Family Estate Planning Attorney*, Francis Burton Doyle, Esq., who is a *Certified Specialist in Tax Law, Probate, Estate Planning and Trust Law*, to create this book for you. Frank designed the *"Pet Protection Trust"* and has contributed to the development of the online forms and pet care guidelines in this book. Once you have completed the online *"Pet Protection Daily Care Guide™"* and the *"Pet Protection Trust"* forms, you will have the peace-of-mind of knowing your pet's welfare is protected.

Ideally, this would be a great time to either complete or update your own estate plan in conjunction with the *"Pet Protection Legal Care Plan"* and then you will be prepared for any unforeseen incapacity issues and/or accidents. When you get your affairs in order, you will have the peace-of-mind of knowing that you have made all the important arrangements (*just-in-case*) for your beloved pet (*and yourself*). In one minute your entire life can change without notice and without warning-- I know because I was one of the people who thought that dealing with death was something that happened to others, certainly not me. This book is part of a series of books I have written based on my own challenges with having four family members die *unexpectedly* in a relatively short period of time, including my 22-year old son, Taylor. I have also experienced the deep sadness that comes from losing a beloved pet. Each of these traumatic events pushed me into to becoming actively involved as an end-of-life planning advocate for others. When you decide to collect your thoughts and complete the legal documents to protect your family (*including your companion pet*), your home and your business, you will then have the security of knowing that you have left an important gift for those left behind.

Planning for your own passing is an uncomfortable subject and one most of us tend to avoid. Sadly, only 3 out of 10 Americans have completed a will and/or trust expressing their final wishes. The majority of people just don't want to think about passing away, about choosing a guardian for a minor child, dealing with being incapacitated or having a life-threatening disease. I encourage you to set up your own estate plan (*if you haven't yet*) and update it regularly. Thankfully, you have chosen to begin this important process by stepping into action and taking care of the business of protecting and providing for the needs of your companion pet. I am committed to helping you and your family to get organized, plan ahead and complete all of your important estate planning documents, including the "*Pet Protection Daily Care Guide*™" and the "*Pet Protection Trust*". This book provides the information and action steps you need to be inspired to get your *Pet Protection Trust* completed. Through my consulting firm, I offer one-on-one coaching services to help you (*from start and finish*) to complete the important planning projects in your life and offer the support you may need during difficult times of forever loss, life change and transitions.

All the best,

Mary G. Anderson
Author

Introduction

The Important Role of Pets in Our Lives

"In his grief over the loss of a dog,
a little boy stands for the first time on tiptoe,
peering into the rueful morrow of manhood.
After this most inconsolable of sorrows
there is nothing life can do to him that he will not be able
somehow to bear."
~James Thurber

We love our pets and the statistics prove that we are committed to providing whatever it takes for their continued health, happiness and welfare. Many a physician has said, *"Get yourself a dog, start walking and you'll begin to lose some weight, get more energy and feel better!"* Pets have been proven to uplift our mood and provide relief from loneliness. Pets offer companionship, they make us laugh, open our hearts, reduce anxiety and satisfy our need to touch and be touched. Research indicates that pet ownership (*especially among the elderly*) impact's the owner's life by lowering blood pressure, reducing depression, lowering the risk of heart disease, shortening the recovery time after a hospitalization and improving concentration and mental attitude. Stories abound about how pets have helped soldiers to cope with PTSD and calmed sick children during difficult medical treatments. Brave dogs are used everyday to protect humans in the armed forces, police and fire departments and during drug enforcement raids. Pets provide life sustaining guidance and security to the blind and handicapped too. It is becoming more and more common that assisted living facilities have specific sections for elders who own companion pets. Many companies are now allowing pet companions to come to work with their owners too! It is not surprising that a pet owner often wants to assure that his or her trusted companion will be well-cared for after the owner's death.

According to *The Humane Society of the United States*, it is estimated that 75-85 million dogs and 74-87 million cats are owned in the United States. Approximately 37-47% of all households in the United States have a dog, and 30-37% have a cat. It seems both dogs and cats are on people's minds when important decisions are made in a family, since 16% of dog owners and 14% of cat owners, claim that their choice of a house or a car was influenced by the fact that they wanted it to be convenient and appropriate for their pet. When it comes to furniture privileges, cats seem to come out winners since in 70% of their households, the cats are allowed to lie on the furniture compared to only 40% of dogs who have been granted similar permission. A majority of pet dogs and cats sleep indoors. In 65% of cat-owning households, the cats are permitted to sleep at night on some of the family member's bed compared with 39% of dogs. Another statistic of interest is that the amount of money spent on cat treats is well in excess of $100 million a year, and while this seems like an astonishing figure, it is tiny compared to the more than $1 billion a year that is spent on dog treats!

Several years ago, the *American Animal Hospital Association* conducted a survey of 1,019 pet owners to determine the role their pets played in their lives. Some 57% said they would want a pet as their only companion if they were stranded on a deserted island; 55% considered themselves a parent to their pets; and 80% selected companionship as the main reason for having pets. Pets are becoming more and more important in our lives. This is borne out by recent research, which shows that 75% of American dog owners view their animals as family members and more than 50% of cat owners feel the same. About 20% of pet owners have actually changed romantic relationships because of disputes over pets. Nearly 40% of pet owners carry pet pictures in their wallets and more than 30% have taken time off work because of sick pets.

The "*Pet Protection Legal Care Plan*" book provides the information you need to understand the legal concepts and practical applications of a "*Pet Protection Trust*". Recent changes in estate law have transformed the way in which courts now deal with domestic animals (*companion pets*). *Family Estate Planning Attorneys* have reported that 90% of their pet-owning clients want and request to make provisions for their animals, either through trusts or some other mechanism. It is not surprising that a pet owner wants to assure that his or her trusted companion is well-cared for after their death. Pet owners are beginning to look for ways to ensure that their pets are safe no matter what. Think about what would happen to your dog and/or cat if you were no longer able to care for him or her? Because pets usually have shorter life spans than the humans who care, protect and love them, it is critical to plan for your pet's future.

Many dogs and cats are found in shelters because their owners became ill or were unable to care for them. Some owners died without leaving plans for their pets' next home. Unfortunately, many of these animals are euthanized because they can't find homes (over 65%). At last estimate over 500,000 companion pets are put to death every year because their owners have passed on without any written care instructions. Sadly, there are a growing number of pets that are neglected or abandoned because an elderly pet owner has dementia and/or can no longer provide the required daily care for the pet. To prevent these outcomes from happening, a pet estate plan is created, which will provide for the proper physical care and financial support for the pet. This is a difficult topic to talk about (*or take action on*) but we all need to remember that our time here is limited. Life is unpredictable, accidents can happen, tragedies befall us and a life threatening diagnosis may occur at any time—remember pet estate planning is about preparing for your pet's future without you, *just-in-case*.

As you can imagine, the whole field of '*animal law*' is expanding. Although shared pet ownership is becoming more common among divorced and separated couples, bitter custody disputes over pets (*like children*) still happen all the time. It's important to note that one of the most common assumptions that people make when thinking about what will happen to their pets after they die, is that a friend or relative will *automatically* take their pet. The fact is, a friend or relative may give it away, take it to a shelter or sell it. If for some unknown reason you don't return from a business trip due to a tragic accident, you alone want to be the person who decides who will ultimately care your pet. This book is designed to save you the time and the expense of an attorney visit by giving you a simple format to document your pet's care needs, personality traits and daily activities.

Chapter 1

Overview of the Pet Estate Planning Process

"There is sorrow enough in the natural way
from men and women to fill our day;
but when we are certain of sorrow in store...
Why do we always arrange for more?
Brothers and sisters I bid you beware
of giving your heart to a dog to tear."
~Rudyard Kipling

Congratulations on choosing to take the time and energy to document your *"Pet Protection Daily Care Guide™"* and the *"Pet Protection Trust"* to provide your care recommendations for the lifelong protection of your companion pet. Here is an overview of the steps you will need to take to complete your pet estate plan and to choose the people, activities and resources that are critical to implementing a successful *Pet Protection Trust*. When a horrible accident occurs or someone dies, everything changes at warp speed. Decisions need to be made. Checks need to be written. Documents need to be found. People need to be called. Because your family and friends are often confused, bereft and in shock, they may argue over the care of your pet and could possibly ignore your request for the animals care. Be prepared "just in case" by completing and distributing a customized *"Pet Protection Daily Care Guide*™*"* and the *"Pet Protection Trust"* for each individual and unique companion pet in your family.

Pet trusts offer pet owners a great deal of flexibility and peace of mind. The best way to make sure your wishes as the pet owner are fulfilled is by making formal arrangements that specifically cover the care of your pet (a *"Pet Protection Trust"*). The primary objective of setting up the *"Pet Protection Legal Care Plan"* is to establish a legal *Pet Protection Trust* that provides the information, guidelines and structure necessary to create a system of checks and balances to protect your companion pet with each member of the pet care team working together. When establishing your *Pet Protection Trust*, the objective includes choosing trustworthy caregivers for your pet and creating a system of checks and balances. The first task to is to choose a trusted person to serve as the *Pet Caregiver/Guardian (and a back-up choice)* to provide a home for your pet and another person to act as the *Pet Financial Caregiver/Trustee (and a back-up choice)* to administer the assets (financial funds) in accordance with the stipulations of the trust.

This book is divided into five chapters each of which collects important information and prepares you to complete the *"Pet Protection Daily Care Guide*™*"* and the *"Pet Protection Trust"*. Most *Family Estate Planning Attorneys* encourage you to name at least one alternative *Pet Caregiver/Guardian* and *Pet Financial Caregiver/Trustee*, just in case your first choice is not willing or able to care for your pet. Unfortunately, we do not always know people as well as we think. Money can have a strange and toxic affect on some humans. You need to choose someone as a *Pet Caregiver/Guardian* (and back-up), who will provide both a "home" and the daily physical care your pet needs. In conjunction with that *Pet Caregiver/Guardian*, you will need to choose someone else to be the *Pet Financial Caregiver/Trustee (and back-up)*, who will manage the assets (financial funds) which have been set aside for the care of the pet. This person will also be responsible for performing periodic home checks on the pet to ensure that they are being cared for in accordance with the stipulations of the "*Pet Protection Trust*".

It's important to review your completed "*Pet Protection Legal Care Plan*" regularly since the caregiver's life and living situation are always subject to change. You may want to have an annual meeting with the important people in your life that you have chosen to protect your pet to let them know about the contents and location of the *Pet Protection Trust* documents (*especially if you update certain sections*). As a responsible pet owner, you provide your pet with food and water, shelter, veterinary care, and love. In order to ensure that your pet will continue to receive this level of care (*if something unexpected happens to you*); it's critical to plan ahead and communicate often. *The Pet Protection Trust* provides, by law, the essential checks and balances to ensure that your pet receives proper care and that the assigned assets (financial funds) that have been left to provide for your pet are used according to your wishes.

Remember if no one in your family can find your "*Pet Protection Daily Care Guide™*" and the "*Pet Protection Trust*", then no matter how much they want to help your pet, they won't be able to follow your wishes. So plan to locate all of your important documents, records, memorabilia, etc. in one place. I recommend choosing one drawer in your desk to define as your "*legacy drawer*" and make sure that all your critical end-of-life planning documents are located in that one place. You might also add a copy of your current estate plan, the "*Pet Protection Legal Care Plan*" (*one for each of your pets*) and any other important documents like copies of your birth certificate, driver's license, deeds, passport, household inventory, etc.

Chapter 2

10 Steps to Completing Your *"Pet Protection Legal Care Plan"*

> "I talk to him when I'm lonesome like;
> and I'm sure he understands.
> When he looks at me so attentively, and gently licks my hands;
> then he rubs his nose on my tailored clothes,
> but I never say naught.
> For the good Lord knows I can buy more clothes,
> but never a friend like that."
> ~W. Dayton Wedgefarth

1. **Identify the *Pet Owner* and the *Pet*:** Complete information about the *Pet Owner,* and *Pet Identification* in Chapter 4, the *"Pet Protection Daily Care Guide™"*.

2. **Choose a Physical Caregiver of Your Pet:** Choose a *Pet Caregiver/ Guardian* to provide a home for your pet *(in case you are ill, hospitalized or have a fatal accident)* and choose a back-up person or an organization *(pet sanctuary, breed rescue organization, etc.),* just in case your original choice of *Pet Caregiver/Guardian* is unable or unwilling to fulfill this responsibility.

3. **Choose a Financial Caregiver of Your Pet:** Choose a *Pet Financial Caregiver/Trustee* to be responsible for managing the assets (financial funds) that have been set aside for the care

of your pet, and to provide oversight that your pet is being properly cared for and the *"Pet Protection Daily Care Guide™"* instructions are being followed. Choose a back-up person or an organization *(pet sanctuary, breed rescue organization, etc.)* just in case your original choice of *Pet Financial Caregiver/ Trustee* is unable or unwilling to fulfill this responsibility. Finally, determine the amount of assets (financial funds) and the location of the account for the physical care of your pet.

4. **Complete the *"Pet Protection Daily Care Guide™"*:** Choose to either complete your documents in the book or online. The *"Pet Protection Daily Care Guide™"* upon completion will provide the details on your pet's physical care plan, which includes detailed information about:

   • Your Pet's Identification
   • Your Pet's Medical Information
   • Your Pet's First Aid Kit and Emergency Preparedness Plan
   • Your Pet's Care Team of Advisors
   • Your Pet's End-of-Life and Funeral Plan

5. **Complete Your *"Pet Protection Trust"* Documents:** When you are ready to complete your own customized *"Pet Protection Daily Care Guide™"* and *"Pet Protection Trust"*, it is easiest to access the forms online. It is best to have the final documents notarized as evidence of their authenticity. You can access a blank template/form online at <u>www.petprotectionlegalcareplan.com</u>.

6. **Distribute a Copy of the Documents:** Plan to distribute a copy of the completed *"Pet Protection Daily Care Guide™"* and the *"Pet Protection Trust"*, to both your *Pet Caregiver/Guardian (and back-up)* and the *Pet Financial Caregiver/Trustee (and back-up)*. You might also want to consider distributing a copy of the *"Pet*

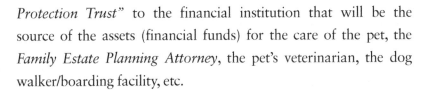

Protection Trust" to the financial institution that will be the source of the assets (financial funds) for the care of the pet, the *Family Estate Planning Attorney*, the pet's veterinarian, the dog walker/boarding facility, etc.

7. **Introduce Your Pet's Physical Care Team:** Introduce your *Pet Caregiver/Guardian* and the *Pet Financial Caregiver/Trustee* to each other and to your pet. Plan to discuss the contents of both the completed *"Pet Protection Daily Care Guide™"* and the *"Pet Protection Trust"* with them and determine the 'phone tree' of calls and action steps that will need to occur in case you have an emergency, unexpected hospitalization and/or fatal accident. Decide who will be the person to step in immediately to take care of your pet.

8. **Plan to Update Your *"Pet Protection Daily Care Guide™"* and *"Pet Protection Trust"* Annually:** If there are any big changes in your life (*e.g. moving, getting a new veterinarian, the health condition of your pet, etc.*), plan to update your *"Pet Protection Legal Care Plan"*. Consider choosing a holiday each year to remind yourself to review the *Pet Protection Trust* to make sure you have a current pet photo and that all the pet care details/instructions are up-to-date. If you do make any changes to the care guide, please let both of your pet caregiver's know about them.

9. **Plan to Complete and/or Update Your Own Estate Plan:** Life is unpredictable. Finishing your *"Pet Protection Daily Care Guide™"* and *"Pet Protection Trust"* is a great first step toward completing your own estate plan. Contact a *Family Estate Planning Attorney* to either establish an estate plan or update your current documents.

10. **Your** *"Legacy Drawer"*: It is critical that your family and friends know where your important emergency and end-of-life planning documents are located in your home or office. It is highly recommend that you pick a drawer in your desk or in a bedroom dresser that will be your "legacy drawer". Plan to put a copy of the *"Pet Protection Daily Care Guide™"* and the *"Pet Protection Trust"* in that drawer. Ideally, the *"legacy drawer"* will also include a copy of your own estate plan, a digital/online list of your passwords, a household inventory, etc. Finally, be sure and let the important people in your life know where you keep these documents.

"Pet Protection Legal Care Plan" **Terminology**

- *"Pet Owner"*= The person who owns the pet (you)
- *"Pet"*= A complete description of the pet including documentation of all forms of ID
- *"Family Estate Planning Attorney"*= The person who is your Estates and Trusts Attorney
- *"Pet Caregiver/Guardian"*= The person who would be the physical caretaker of your pet
- *"Pet Financial Caregiver/Trustee"*= The person who would manage the assets (financial funds) that will be used to care for your pet and monitor the care of the pet
- *"Assets (Financial Funds)"*= The financial account that has been designated for use for the physical care of your pet
- *"Pet Protection Daily Care Guide™"*= A guide to the physical care of the pet including daily activities, medical information, pet support advisors, emergency plans, etc.
- *"Advanced Health Care Directive for Pets"*= A form which allows the *Pet Caregiver/Guardian* to provide emergency medical care for your pet if you are unable to provide it due to incapacity, etc.

- *"Pet Protection Trust"*= A legal document that protects the life of your pet and provides continued care for them
- *"Notary of the Public"*= A person who authorizes the authenticity of the *"Pet Protection Trust"*
- *"Legacy Drawer*™*"*= The place/location of all of your important estate planning documents

Chapter 3

How to Identify the *Pet Care Support Team* Members and Determine Their Responsibilities

"This soldier, I realized, must have had friends at home and in his regiment; yet he lay there deserted by all, except his dog.
I looked on, unmoved, at battles,
which decided the future of nations.
Tearless, I had given orders, which brought death to thousands.
Yet here I was stirred, profoundly stirred, stirred to tears, and by what? By the grief of one dog."
~Napoleon Bonaparte, on finding a dog beside the body of his dead master, licking his face and howling, on a moonlit field after a battle. This scene haunted Napoleon until his own death.

Let's get started! The goal of completing a *"Pet Protection Trust"* is to provide the essential information and directions to ensure that your pet receives the proper care in the event that you cannot provide that care. We are committed to supporting you in providing this end-of-life roadmap to provide the necessary protection to ensure the continued care of your companion pet. Without your direction in a proper *Pet Protection Trust* document, your family and friends will have to make last minute decisions about your pet's needs when they are each filled with grief and have so many other details to handle. Here is a brief overview of the different parts of creating a *"Pet Protection Legal Care Plan"*:

1. Identify the *"Pet Owner"*, *"Family Estate Planning Attorney"*, choose a *"Pet Financial Caregiver/Guardian"* and a *"Pet Financial Caregiver/Trustee"* to provide ongoing care for your pet.

2. Identify the *"Pet"* and complete the *"Pet Protection Daily Care Guide™"*.

3. Complete the *"Pet Protection Trust"* template with your pet's information (online) and have it notarized.

Overview and Identity of the Pet Owner and Suggested Responsibilities

It is important to establish who the owner of the pet is, especially because pets are legally classified as property. Often in the confusion that accompanies a pet owner's unexpected illness, accident, or death, pets may be overlooked. In some cases, companion pets are discovered in a person's home many days after an unexpected tragedy. To prevent this from happening to your pet, take the simple precaution of completing a customized *"Pet Protection Legal Care Plan"* with the details about your emergency plan. In conjunction with having your pet's ID up-to-date, you will also be prepared for the unexpected.

Contact Information: *Pet Owner*
Name:
Address *(Street, City, State, & Zip Code):*
Phone:
Email:

Suggested responsibilities of the *Pet Owner* include:

- Plan to complete one *"Pet Protection Legal Care Plan"* (which includes both a *"Pet Protection Daily Care Guide*™*"* and a *"Pet Protection Trust"*) per pet and have it notarized.
- Plan to communicate the details of your *"Pet Protection Daily Care Guide*™*"* with each of your selected caregivers.
- Plan to distribute a copy of your completed *"Pet Protection Legal Care Plan"* to your designated *Pet Caregiver/ Guardian* (and back-up) and *Pet Financial Caregiver/ Trustee* (and back-up). You may also wish to notify others about the completed *Pet Protection Trust* documents such as your pet's veterinarian, dog walker, groomer, boarding facility, family members, neighbors, friends and/or your *Family Estate Planning Attorney (include a copy with your estate plan documents).*
- If you or your extended family own any additional property and/or a residence (e.g. cabin, vacation home, etc.) consider keeping a copy of the *"Pet Protection Legal Care Plan"* at that residence too.
- If you travel regularly with your pet, you may want to take an abbreviated copy of the plan with you on your trip.
- Another recommendation is to consider scanning the completed *"Pet Protection Legal Care Plan"* pages onto your laptop, smart phone or tablet for immediate access too.

Contact Information: *Pet Owner*

Name:

Firm Address *(Street, City, State, & Zip Code):*

Phone:

Email:

Overview and Identity of the Family Estate Planning Attorney and Suggested Responsibilities

How to Choose a *Family Estate Planning Attorney*

When you choose a *Family Estate Planning Attorney* it is important that you feel comfortable that the professional you select will be available to represent your intent and values as noted in your "*Pet Protection Legal Care Plan*" and/ or your own estate plan. Even though you do not need to hire an attorney to complete the *Pet Protection Trust* we have created, it is highly recommended that you have a qualified *Family Estate Planning Attorney* review the completed *Pet Protection Trust* and include it with your own estate planning documents

Tips on Choosing a *Family Estate Planning Attorney*

Remember that one day your legal advisor will answer questions and ultimately work with your heirs to manage your affairs and interests after you are deceased. Here are some ideas on how to begin your search for the best *Family Estate Planning Attorney* for your needs:

- Ask a trusted friend and family member for a referral
- Ask your bank officer
- Ask your financial advisor
- Ask your stockbroker

When you have a consensus of names, begin the research and selection process by looking over each firm's current website and review the following information:

- How long has the *Family Estate Planning Attorney* been in practice?
- What kind of law (specialty) does the attorney practice (*what percentage of their law practice is devoted to estate and trusts law and litigation*)?
- Request references and review any client testimonials and determine if there is a fee for an initial in-person consultation.

Remember, the ultimate goal of choosing a *Family Estate Planning Attorney* and completing your own estate plan is so that you, your family, your pet and your hard earned assets will be protected under the law for years to come.

Suggested responsibilities of the *Family Estate Planning Attorney* include:

- Request that the attorney review the completed "*Pet Protection Legal Care Plan*" (which includes both a "*Pet Protection Daily Care Guide*™" and a "*Pet Protection Trust*") one document per pet
- Request that the attorney add the completed and notarized "*Pet Protection Legal Care Plan*" (which includes both a "*Pet Protection Daily Care Guide*™" and a "*Pet Protection Trust*" to your estate plan)

Contact Information: *Family Estate Planning Attorney*
Name:
Firm Address *(Street, City, State, & Zip Code):*
Phone:
Email/Website:

Overview and Identity of the Pet Caregiver/Guardian and Suggested Responsibilities

How to Choose a *Pet Caregiver/Guardian*

The *Pet Caregiver/Guardian* is essentially the person that you have chosen to care for your pet when you cannot. He or she will be responsible for the daily care and all the decisions made on behalf of your pet's physical welfare. The *Pet Caregiver/Guardian* will handle the pet's daily activities including the pet's diet, exercise routine, medical treatments and ultimately, even their death. The designated caregiver *(and back up)* should be expected to follow your wishes and directives regarding the care of your pet and must be willing to assume all of the responsibilities associated with the physical care of your pet. The *Pet Caregiver/Guardian* will keep the pet, generally in their home, and must carry out the pet owner's instructions. Some potential caregivers will be reticent to accept such a large responsibility. Reasons may include that they don't have enough time for the required care of the animal or pet care is just too expensive and/or messy and finally some potential caregivers are concerned about allergies.

Tips on Choosing a *Pet Caregiver/Guardian*

First, consider choosing someone who lives close by who could step in to take care of your pet temporarily, in the hours, days, or weeks after an emergency, and/or who would consider adopting your pet should you become incapacitated or pass away. Your primary *(and back-up)* choice for *Pet Caregiver/Guardian* may be a responsible friend, relative or neighbor who loves animals and will agree to serve as the *Pet Caregiver/Guardian*. Ideally, there should always be a successor *(back-up) Pet Caregiver/Guardian* selected to ensure physical care if the original choice for *Pet Caregiver/Guardian* is unwilling or unable to assume care for the surviving pet. Select at least two people who are willing and able to care for your pet in the event of an emergency or your death.

Ideally, the *Pet Caregiver/Guardian* you have named could immediately take custody and control of your pet if necessary. Don't assume the person or organization you want to name as the physical caregiver/guardian—even if it's your neighbor or best friend—is willing to take on this important responsibility. Always ask and plan to have specific conversations with these people and give them the opportunity to say no. Although this is not the answer you may want to hear, it is important that you get an honest answer as opposed to one based on feelings of obligation.

It's important to remember that even though a friend or relative promised you a couple of years back that they love cats (or dogs) and would be happy to care for your pet too. It's not enough that this person verbally promised to take in your animal, plan to document the agreement. The best choice for the *Pet Caregiver/Guardian* will be someone who is dedicated to following your instructions in the *"Pet Protection Daily Care Guide™"*. Another issue to consider as the *pet owner* is if you would like to keep certain animals together because they were raised together or have otherwise bonded, make sure to include this important instruction in the *"Pet Protection Trust"* document and care plan; it will not happen automatically. The ability to keep pets together can have a significant impact on the choice of the *Pet Caregiver/Guardian* as well.

If you're not able to locate a responsible person both willing and able to take on the role of *Pet Caregiver/Guardian*, you are not without options. The *Pet Caregiver/Guardian* that you choose to watch over your pet can be a person or an organization. If you cannot find a friend, relative, or neighbor to care for your pet, consider contacting your veterinarian, local pet sitters, animal rescue groups and no-kill sanctuaries as possible resources to contact to help you locate a potential *Pet Caregiver/Guardian* who meets your pet's unique care requirements. Remember, if you cannot find a *Pet Caregiver/Guardian* that fits your needs, there are other options available for you to consider including programs that exist across the country that allow you to leave your pet to a trustworthy organization after you pass away. Many shelters and veterinary schools now offer continuing pet care programs, where you pay an enrollment fee or give an annual donation to the organization, and they promise to care for your companion pet upon your death. If a pet organization assumes this role, the *Pet Protection Trust* document should include directions about the adoption and transfer of the pet.

Please note the same person or organization named as the *Pet Caregiver/Guardian* can also be in charge of the funds outlined below for the care of your pet, however appointing a different person as the *Pet Financial Caregiver/Trustee* or organization to each role will create a system of shared responsibility which will further protect your beloved pet.

One important feature of a *Pet Protection Trust* is that it can take effect before your death, if necessary, in case you were to become hospitalized or incapacitated and unable to care for your pet. A growing number of pets are euthanized because they have outlived their owner's ability to care for them. By creating a *Pet Protection Trust* you can ensure that you're beloved dog, cat, bird or any other pet, is provided for in the manner you feel is best. It's also important for your designated *Pet Caregiver/Guardian (and back-up)* to have access to your home including a set of keys and a copy of the alarm codes to access your home in case of an emergency. The *Pet Caregiver/ Guardian* should also have a copy of the completed and notarized *"Pet Protection Legal Care Plan"*, which includes a copy of the *"Advanced Health Care Directive for Pets"*. All of the permanent care provisions for your pet will be documented in the *"Pet Protection Daily Care Guide*™*"* (see Chapter 4) and these directions will create and ensure a forever safe, comfortable and secure emergency plan for your pet.

Suggested responsibilities of the *Pet Caregiver/Guardian include*:

- The *Pet Caregiver/Guardian* should be expected to follow your wishes and directives regarding the physical care of your pet and must be willing to assume all of the responsibilities associated with caring for your pet as outlined in the *"Pet Protection Daily Care Guide*™*"*
- The *Pet Caregiver/Guardian* is responsible to provide 100% of the pet's physical care when and if the *Pet Owner* cannot *(including feeding, exercise, medical treatments, etc. and ultimately, even their passing)*
- The *Pet Caregiver/Guardian* is responsible for the daily care, protection and all the decisions made on behalf of your pet's health and welfare
- The *Pet Caregiver/Guardian* will also keep the pet, generally in their home, and if a pet organization assumes this role, the *Pet Protection Trust* document should include directions about adoption

Information About the *Pet Caregiver/Guardian*

Contact Information: *Pet Caregiver/Guardian*

Name:

Address *(Street, City, State, & Zip Code)*:

Phone:

Email:

Contact Information: *Pet Caregiver/Guardian* (back-up)

Name:

Address *(Street, City, State, & Zip Code)*:

Phone:

Email:

Overview and Identity of the Pet Financial Caregiver/ Trustee and Suggested Responsibilities

How to Choose a *Pet Financial Caregiver/Trustee*

Part of the financial and legal pet protection planning process includes choosing someone to manage and allocate the assets (financial funds) you have set aside for the pet's lifetime care. This person is often a referred to as the *Pet Financial Caregiver/Trustee*. The *Pet Financial Caregiver/Trustee* (and back up*)* is the person that you choose to administer and manage the monies that have been secured in the *Pet Protection Trust* you are now creating for your pet's long-term care, when and if you can no longer provide it for them. The *Pet Financial Caregiver/Trustee* is responsible for all the financial decisions that will be made on behalf of your pet to insure their health and welfare in your absence. The *Pet Financial Caregiver/Trustee* is also the person who will provide oversight for your pet's continued care in your absence by distributing the assets (financial funds) that you have set aside to provide for the physical day-to-day care of your pet.

Tips on Choosing the *Pet Financial Caregiver/Trustee*

When choosing your *Pet Financial Caregiver/Trustee* (and back-up) you might want to look toward choosing a trusted family member or friend of whom you would be confident with them managing a sum of monies and the other fiduciary responsibilities related to the proper care of your pet. Ideally, the *Pet Caregiver/Guardian* and the *Pet Financial Caregiver/Tr*ustee are a team that provides a 'check and balance' system together to make sure your pet is both cared and provided for financially in the manner you have requested for the duration of the pet's life.

The *Pet Financial Caregiver/Trustee* will be responsible for managing the assets (financial funds) that you have set aside in a bank account for your pet's care *(in case you are unable to provide it)*. You will want to choose a *Pet Financial Caregiver/Trustee* that you both trust and have confidence that this person will manage the *Pet Protection Trust* funds appropriately to provide the best care possible for your pet. Where will your pet live? Does your potential *Pet Financial Caregiver/Trustee* live within 10-20 miles of your chosen *Pet Caregiver/Guardian*? The geographic proximity of these two caregivers will be important for the ease and flow of caring for your pet. Are you comfortable with the potential *Pet Financial Caregiver/Trustee* having the responsibility of checking in on the *Pet Caregiver/Guardian* from time to time to evaluate the ongoing physical care of your pet? Typically, this would also be the time that the assets (financial funds) would be given to the physical caregiver for the continued care of the pet.

When choosing a potential financial caregiver, consider whether this person has the time, willingness and ability to manage the pet care budget, financial planning and distribution of the assets (financial funds) that you have put aside for your pet's care according to the instructions in your *"Pet Protection Daily Care Guide*™*"*. How flexible is your potential *Pet Financial Caregiver/Trustee's* daily schedule? If you were to be in an accident, would the financial caregiver be able to step in immediately to provide the required financial oversight to assist and support the physical caregiver?

Suggested responsibilities of the *Pet Financial Caregiver/Trustee* include:

- The *Pet Financial Caregiver/Trustee* has the primary responsibility of managing the bank account and/or assets (financial funds) for the pet's physical care.
- The *Pet Financial Caregiver/Trustee* determines the spending plan and to what extent the assets (financial funds) will be available to cover the cost of services such as veterinary insurance, liability insurance in case the pet bites or injures someone, etc.
- The *Pet Financial Caregiver/Trustee* has the responsibility of setting up a distribution schedule of payments *(e.g. weekly, monthly or bi-annual payments)* to the *Pet Caregiver/Guardian* for the pet's needs and daily care.
- The *Pet Financial Caregiver/Trustee* determines the method the *Pet Caregiver/Guardian* should use to document the pet care expenses for reimbursement.
- The *Pet Financial Caregiver/Trustee* sets up a schedule with the *Pet Caregiver/Guardian* for home visits and/or another monitoring system to assure the proper ongoing care of the pet.
- The *Pet Financial Caregiver/Trustee* works in conjunction with the *Pet Caregiver/Guardian* to make any end-of-life medical care decisions about the pet.

- The *Pet Financial Caregiver/Trustee* determines in conjunction with the *Pet Caregiver/Guardian*, the final disposition of the pet (burial, cremation, etc.) and the final distribution of any remaining assets (financial funds) per the *"Pet Protection Trust"*.

- Finally, the *Pet Financial Caregiver/Trustee* is the person who will distribute any funds that are left over after your pet passes away and will appropriate those funds according to your wishes, as outlined in in Chapter 5, the *"Pet Protection Trust"*. The majority of *Pet Owners* choose to leave the remaining funds after a pets' death to an animal charity and/or the *Pet Caregiver/Guardian* and/ or the *Pet Financial Caregiver/Trustee*.

Information About the *Pet Financial Caregiver/Trustee*

Contact Information: *Pet Financial Caregiver/Trustee*

Name:

Address *(Street, City, State, & Zip Code)*:

Phone:

Email:

Contact Information: *Pet Financial Caregiver/Trustee* (back-up)

Name:

Address (*Street, City, State, & Zip Code*):

Phone:

Email:

Location of completed *Advanced Health Care Directive for Pet*:

Information and Location of Assets (Financial Funds) to Provide for Your Pet's Care

As the *Pet Owner*, you will need to analyze the appropriate sum of assets (financial funds) to leave in the care of the *Pet Financial Caregiver/Trustee* for your pet's care. The *Pet Financial Caregiver/Trustee* will need to both manage and distribute the assets (financial funds) to the physical caregiver (*Pet Caregiver/Guardian*) to provide the standard-of-living you would like to maintain for your pet. The *"Pet Protection Trust"* in conjunction with the *"Pet Protection Daily Care Guide™"* (see Chapter 4) will delineate your expectations to ensure a forever safe and comfortable home for your pet.

Remember that the appropriate amount of assets (financial funds) to leave for your pet's care may vary widely depending on your pet's age and physical condition. Be aware that if you set aside an amount in the *Pet Protection Trust* that is unreasonably high that a family member or other beneficiary could challenge it in court, and a judge may decide to reduce it. Although funding (putting funds in place now in an account) is optional, it is highly recommended. Funds can be a fixed amount or a percentage of an insurance policy, bank account, 401(k), or even a portion of the sale of a home. Consider also that the cost of owning a companion pet, either a cat or a dog, can vary widely, depending on the type, mix, and size of your pet. Keep in mind; the first year of a pet's life will cost more due to vaccinations, spaying and neutering fees, and first time accessories. Older pets can cost more because they may require more visits to the veterinarian due to illness and/or accidents.

After completing an analysis of your pet's needs (see the *Pet Caregiver/Guardian Fund Allotment Worksheet* below), you can easily open a savings account at your bank. After you have signed your completed

"*Pet Protection Legal Care Plan*" and it has been notarized, you will need to take a copy of the form to your bank. The bank should then change the name on your savings account from your name as an individual to your name as Trustee of the *Pet Protection Trust*. As the pet owner, you will continue to have 100% access to your funds while you are alive. If you pass away or are incapacitated, the *Pet Financial Caregiver/Trustee* will be the legal owner of the balance in the account to only use the funds for the care of your pet per your instructions.

Finally, the primary two responsibilities of the *Pet Financial Caregiver/ Trustee* are to distribute the funds as needed to the *Pet Caregiver/ Guardian* and to make sure that the trust money is being spent appropriately on the animal's daily care and not for any other reason. As the *Pet Owner* you will need to analyze the appropriate sum of assets (financial funds) to leave in an account of the *Pet Financial Caregiver/Trustee* for your pet's care. Here is a one simple method of analyzing the financial needs of your pet:

Pet Caregiver/Guardian Fund Allotment Worksheet
How to Determine the Sum of Assets (financial funds) to Leave for the Care of Your Pet

Estimate amounts spent *each month* on:
Monthly Allowance: *Physical Care of the Pet*

Cost of Food	$____
Cost of Medications/Supplements:	$____
Cost of Routine Veterinarian Visits	$____
Cost of Flea/Tick/Worm Treatment	$____
Cost of Special Medical Visits/Chronic Health Issues	$____

Cost of Pet Medical Insurance $_____

Cost of Pet Liability Insurance $_____

Cost of Grooming and Nail Care $_____

Cost of Toys/Recreation/Treats $_____

Cost of Accessories (toys, leashes, collars, bedding, etc.) $_____

Cost of Kennels/Crates $_____

Cost of Travel/Airline Service for Pets $_____

Cost of Boarding/Sitting $_____

Cost of Pet Walker $_____

Cost of Obedience Training $_____

Compensation for *Pet Caregiver/Guardian* $_____

Compensation for *Pet Financial Caregiver/Trustee* $_____

Monthly Allowance: *End-of-Life Care Expenses*

Hospice Care for Animals $_____

Pet Crypts, Vaults and Coffins $_____

Pet Cemetery Plot $_____

Pet Burial/Cremation Services $_____

Funeral/Celebration of Life $_____

Support of a Pet Charity $_____

Other $_____

Other $_____

TOTAL: Multiply by 12 for ANNUAL AMOUNT $_____

Additional Tips on How to Determine a Monthly Care Allowance for Your Pet:

- Based on the sum that you decide upon to "fund the trust", you need to then decide how much and how often you want the *Pet Financial Caregiver/Trustee* to distribute funds to the *Pet Caregiver/Guardian*, for your pet's care *(a base amount, subject to additional distributions for extraordinary expenses)*.

- Consider compensation you deem appropriate for the *Pet Caregiver/Guardian's* and/or the *Pet Financial Caregiver/ Trustee's* time.
- Consider providing an "*emergency fund*" for immediate cash in case of an unexpected medical emergency that might be unforeseen in your current customized pet care plan.
- Depending on the number of years you estimate your pet will live *(based on current age and breed)* you may want to consider the possibility of inflation *(if you set up and put the assets (financial funds) into the trust while you are alive, you can always add or remove funds at any time)*.

The Amount of Assets (Financial Funds) You Want to Leave in Trust for Your Pet's Care

- The amount of funds for the pet's care shall be $_____ (Per Month/Per Year/Other _____)
- The *Pet Financial Caregiver/Trustee* must distribute to the *Pet Caregiver/Guardian* the assets (financial funds) as follows: (Yearly/As needed/Other _____)
- Compensation for the *Pet Caregiver/Guardian (optional)* shall be $_____ (Per Month/Per Year/Other _____)
- Compensation for the *Pet Financial Caregiver/Trustee (optional)* shall be $_____ (Per Month/Per Year/Other _____)

Location of Assets (financial funds)

Where shall the assets (financial funds) come from?

Bank Account #_____

Life Insurance Policy #_____

Property #_____

Other _____

Contact Information: Location of Assets *(financial funds)*
Name of Bank and/or Financial Institution:
Name of Bank Manager:
Account #:
Address *(Street, City, State, & Zip Code)*:
Phone:
Email/Website:
Location of completed *Durable Power of Attorney for the Pet's Financial Funds*:

Distribution of Property When the Pet Passes Away
(Upon Trust Termination):

Finally, when your pet passes away, it is the responsibility of the *Pet Financial Caregiver/Trustee* to distribute the assets (financial funds) that may be remaining in the bank according to the *"Pet Protection Trust"*. In general, the *Pet Financial Caregiver/Trustee* has the responsibility to manage the *Pet Protection Trust* assets (financial funds) during the pet's lifetime and then upon the death of the pet, the *Pet Financial Caregiver/Trustee* will distribute the remaining *Pet Protection Trust* assets (financial funds) to the designated beneficiaries.

As the *Pet Owner* you may want to consider leaving the remaining funds to the *Pet Caregiver/Guardian, Pet Financial Caregiver/ Trustee, Pet Hospice* or another organization that you would choose to support. If you want to choose several beneficiaries, most *Family*

Estate Planning Attorneys recommend that you indicate a percentage of the remaining funds instead of a dollar amount.

List of beneficiaries:

Name/Organization:
Address *(Street, City, State, & Zip Code)*:
Phone:
Email:
Specific amount, item, or percent of item:

Name/Organization:
Address *(Street, City, State, & Zip Code)*:
Phone:
Email:
Specific amount, item, or percent of item:

Name/Organization:
Address *(Street, City, State, & Zip Code)*:
Phone:
Email:
Specific amount, item, or percent of item:

Chapter 4

How to Complete the
"Pet Protection Daily Care Guide™"

"There's a stone I had made for Luke at the
top of the road on the hill,
where the pasture opens wide and the setting sun highlights the
words carved into its face. *"That'll do, Luke, that'll do."*
The words are said to working dogs all over the world when
the chores are done and the flock is settled:
"That'll do dog, come home now, your work is done."
Luke's work is done too. He took my heart and ran with it,
and he's running still, fast and strong, a piece of my heart
bound up with his, forever."
~Patricia McConnell, *For the Love of a Dog*

This chapter is dedicated to providing a complete description of your
pet including both a physical description including notes on their
unique personality traits, daily activities and medical information.
The *"Pet Protection Daily Care Guide™"* is designed to identify and
document the daily routine of your pet. Completing this section of the
book will create a customized, individualized and unique daily care
plan for your pet. This care guide requires that you take the time to
document and capture the one-of-kind personality and behavior of
your pet. There are many questions listed here to help you think about

your companion pet's daily routine and their specific *(if any)* location for sleeping, eating, baths, grooming, walking or exercise (including how well the pet interacts with other animals, special play activities and more). Please feel free to add any additional information pages to this section of the book that would be helpful to the *Pet Caregiver/ Guardian* and/or the *Pet Financial Caregiver/Trustee.* Here is a summary of the contents of the *"Pet Protection Daily Care Guide™"* which includes the following information:

I. Your Pet's ID Information

- Your *Pet ID Tag* Information and a *Current Photo of Your Pet*
- Your *Emergency Wallet Card* and *Home Pet Alert ID*

II. Your Pet's Physical Description and Behavior Characteristics

- Your Pet's Behavioral Characteristics
- Your Pet's Likes and Dislikes

III. Your Pet's Daily Schedule and Activities

- Your Pet's Behavioral Characteristics
- Your Pet's Home Environment and Activities
- Your Pet's Diet & Feeding Schedule
- Your Pet's Exercise, Socialization and Play Schedule
- Your Pet's Sleep Schedule
- Your Pet's Grooming Schedule
- Location of Other Pet Supplies and the *"Pet Protection Trust"* Documents

IV. Your Pet's Medical Information

- Your Pet's Medical Information/History, Prescriptions and Vaccination Schedule
- Your *Pet's Emergency Preparedness Plan*

- Location of the *Pet First Aid Kit* and the *Pet Emergency Preparedness Disaster Supply Kit*
- Your Pet's *"Advanced Health Care Directive for Pet"* for emergency care
- List of Health Care Tips for Your Pet

V. Your Pet's Care Support Advisor List
- Contact List: Pet Care Support Advisors

VI. Your Pet's End-of-Life Plan and Care Instructions
- Your Pet's Hospice Care Plan
- Your Pet's Funeral/Memorial Plan
- Final Distribution of Assets (Financial Funds) and/or the Philanthropic Legacy
- Pet Caregiver Agreement and Acknowledgement of *"Pet Customized Care Agreement™"*

VII. Your *Pet Caregiver/Guardian* and *Pet Financial Caregiver/ Trustee Agreement* and Acknowledgement of the *"Pet Protection Daily Care Guide™"* Form

"Pet Protection Daily Care Guide™"

I. Your Pet's Identification (*ID*) Information and Physical Description

The Importance of Identifying Your Pet

Millions of companion animals are dropped off at animal shelters nationwide every year. Of these, only 2% of the cats and 15-20% of the dogs are reunited with their owners. As you begin to complete your *"Pet Protection Legal Care Plan"*, it is very important to identify your pet in detail to deter the possibility of a *Pet Caregiver/Guardian* from replacing the original pet in order to illegally extend asset (financial fund) distributions or benefits. There are several methods to employ to accurately describe and identify your pet. Responsible pet owners need to use one or more of the following pet identification methods to ensure the *"Pet Protection Trust"* is secure and also to allow your pet, if ever lost, to be safely returned home. Here are three methods of identification to consider using to ensure your pet's safety:

Method 1:
Pet Collars and Identification (ID) Tags

Collars and tags are a reliable way to identify your pet should they become lost. Make sure your dog or cat always wears a collar with a current identification tag and that the tag is readable. A collar worn for purposes of identification should remain on the dog or cat as long as it is in a situation where he or she could become lost. Pet supply catalogs and stores, veterinary offices, and animal shelters often have forms to order personalized ID tags. The tag should include:

- Pet's name
- Owner's name and address and telephone numbers (*day and evening*)
- List of any Medical problems requiring medication
- Veterinarian's name and number
- Current Rabies vaccination information
- Reward offer should pet become lost

Additional tags commonly worn on the pet's collar include a rabies tag, dog or cat city license tag and an individualized identification tag. Plan to check your pet's tags regularly, as they may become lost, or unreadable with wear. In addition to identification tags, you may use an indelible pen to write a phone number on the collar itself or you can order broad buckle nylon collars with the pet's name and your phone number stitched into the collar online. Many animals may get lost when the pet owner moves across town or the country. If you have moved or are planning to move, use masking tape to cover the current tag or consider purchasing an instant tag, available at most pet supply stores. Always put a temporary tag on your pet when you move to a different home which should include a relative or friend's telephone number. There are several national tag registries that can be contacted if you lose or find a pet. If required, the *Pet Caregiver/ Guardian* will need to order a new set of tags with all the changed information for your pet's new home.

Method 2:
Pet Microchip Identification System

Micro-chipping involves a veterinarian implanting a tiny capsule *(the tiny chip is about the size of a grain of rice)* under the pet's skin, in mammals, usually between the shoulder blades. Microchips can be used on dogs, cats, ferrets, birds, and other companion pets. The owner provides the current contact and alternate contact information in the event the pet becomes lost. When a pet is found, any agency with a scanner, including many animal care and control agencies, veterinary clinics, and research labs, can quickly identify the code that links the animal to its owner through a national database.

Method 3:
Pet Tattoo Identification System

Tattooing is a permanent ID system that involves marking a code on the skin of the pet. The finder of the lost pet calls a national database that uses the code to obtain the owner's current address and phone number. Each registry has its own coding system. Many veterinarians are now using a tattoo to indicate that a companion pet has been neutered or spayed.

Pet Identity Information

Name of Pet
Home/Address (*Street, City, State, & Zip Code*):
Pet Owner's Phone

Pet's Individualized Identification Tag Information

- What is your pet's city license tag #?
- What is your pet's rabies vaccine tag #?
- Is your pet micro-chipped? What is your pet's microchip #?
- Does your pet have an ID tattoo?

Important Emergency and Disaster Identification for Your Pet

To begin to be prepared for an emergency or disaster, it is critical to have the proper ID for your pet, your *"Home Pet Alert ID"* (*as the household with a pet on premise*) and your *"Emergency Pet Alert Wallet Card"* to carry with you as the pet owner. Start with making sure your neighbors, friends, and relatives know how many pets you have and the names and contact numbers of the individuals who have agreed to serve as the pet caregivers.

"Emergency Pet Alert Wallet Card"

Keep a copy of the '*Emergency Pet Alert Wallet Card*' in both your wallet and another copy in the glove box of your car. The '*Emergency Pet Alert Wallet Card*' should list the names and phone numbers of your emergency *Pet Caregiver/Guardian* and/or *Pet Financial Caregiver/Trustee* in case you have a car accident or other unexpected emergency. If you, as the pet owner, become ill suddenly, injured and/or require emergency services, the 'Emergency Pet Alert Wallet Card' will notify emergency personnel of the number and types of pets living at your home who will need immediate care, along with whom to contact. In addition, the wallet card should include any vital information for the special needs of the pet, such as allergies, blood type, and who will be caring for the pet in the event of illness or injury etc. Because pets need care daily and will need *immediate* attention should you become incapacitated; the importance of making these informal arrangements for temporary caregiving cannot be overemphasized. Here is an example of the information to include in your 'Emergency Pet Alert Wallet Card':

EMERGENCY PET ALERT WALLET CARD
In case of emergency, please call my pets' backup caregivers (see reverse side).

_____
Name of Pet Owner, Phone

_____
Address of Pet Owner

Name of Pet_____ Type of Animal _____
Name of Pet _____Type of Animal _____

~~~~~~~~~~~~~~~~~~~~~~~~~~~~~~~~~~~ *(fold here)*

EMERGENCY PET ALERT WALLET CARD
In case of emergency, please call my pets' backup caregiver below. I have _____ pets in my home.

_____
Name of Pet Caregiver, Phone

_____
Name of Pet Veterinarian, Phone

Home Pet Alert ID

Police & Fire Home Alert for Your Pet's Safety:

No one wants to think about preparing for an emergency situation at your residence but just in case of such an event, it is important to have a notification that you have a pet living with you. For instance, in case of a fire, pets cannot fend for themselves and need to be taken or let out by humans. In the event that you are not home during an emergency or are forced to evacuate before you can bring your pet, make sure you have a clear *'In Case of Emergency'* notice near your home's exits to ensure your pet will never be forgotten. Here is an example of a home/residence emergency card to alert rescue personnel that you have pet living in your home:

Plan to affix these removable *"in case of emergency"* notices on both the inside of your front and back doors and/or windows to specify how many and what types of pet(s) you have living in your home. Ideally, these notices will alert emergency-response personnel during a fire or other home emergency to look for and evacuate your pet safely. Avoid using stickers as they are often very hard-to-remove and may be left behind by former residents, so firefighters and other emergency personnel may assume that the sticker is outdated or, worse, risk their lives trying to find a pet no longer in the house.

Your Pet's Emergency Identification Information

- Location of the pet's ***Emergency Pet Alert Wallet Card***'—to alert emergency personnel in case of a car accident, emergency medical issue, etc. that there is a pet at your residence that needs care
- Location of your pet's ***Home Pet Alert ID***—to alert emergency personnel in case of fire, flood, earthquake, etc., that there is a pet living inside your residence that needs care
- Location of the pet's "*Advanced Health Care Directive for Pets*" form
- Location of the *Pet's First Aid Kit*
- Location of the *Pet Disaster Supply Kit* in case of an emergency or disaster
- Pet owner's name, address and telephone numbers *(day and evening)*
- List of your pet's medical problem(s) requiring medication
- Pet's veterinarian and number
- Reward offer should pet become lost

II. Your Pet's Physical Description and Behavior Characteristics

- What is your pet's name? Do you have any nicknames for your pet?
- What is your pet's date of birth (*if known*)? What is the approximate age of your pet?
- What sex is your pet?
- Is your pet neutered/spayed?
- Is your pet declawed (*cat only*)?
- What breed is your pet?

- Who is your pet's breeder (*if applicable*)?
- Was your pet recued from a shelter?
- What is your pet's size and physical description (*include coloring/markings, scars, hair length, etc.*)
- As the pet owner, do you have any additional information about your pet's overall personality to share?

(Place a current photo of your pet here)

Personality Characteristics and Behavior Traits of Your Pet

Please describe your pet's personality overall, including such details as how they act around strangers, children, other animals, being crated, visiting the vet, etc. Please describe your pet's best behavior traits (*e.g. gentle with kids, never bites, loves the dog park, calm with strangers, etc.*). Now add a list of the any more challenging behavior traits/habits too (*e.g. excessive barking, jumping up on guests, chewing on things, running away, digging holes, pulls on the leash, sneaks treats, etc.*). Put everything in writing, including things you don't want to happen if and when your pet needed to be living with the *Pet Caregiver/ Guardian*. For instance, some owners would not want their pets to be placed in a caged environment or separated from one another. Please provide detailed notes about your pet's unique personality here:

Pet Behavior Characteristics (*please check all that apply to your pet*):

- Quiet/Reserved
- Aloof
- Separation anxiety
- Outgoing/Friendly
- Playful
- Destructive
- Cat compatible
- Dog compatible
- Cat Aggressive
- Dog Aggressive
- Escape Artist
- Claws/Bites playfully
- Sprays/Marks
- Independent
- Protective
- Enjoys grooming
- Obedience trained
- Walks well on leash, no pulling
- Rides well in car
- Crate trained
- Carrier trained
- Travels well in car (*longer trips*)
- Uses scratching post (*cat only*)
- Uses litter box indoors (cat only)

Your Pet's Likes/Dislikes (*circle one*)

- Men: Don't know—Likes—Neutral—Dislikes
- Women: Don't know—Likes—Neutral—Dislikes
- Children: Don't know—Likes—Neutral—Dislikes

- Cats: Don't know—Likes—Neutral—Dislikes
- Dogs: Don't know—Likes—Neutral—Dislikes
- Strangers Don't know—Likes—Neutral—Dislikes
- Noises: Don't know—Likes—Neutral—Dislikes
- Other: Don't know—Likes—Neutral—Dislikes

If "Other", please specify:

Indicate any other dislikes and/or fears *(e.g. vacuum, broom, thunder, sensitive areas to avoid, best way to pick up, etc.)*

III. Your Pet's Daily Schedule and Activities

Your Pet's Home Environment and Activities

- Is this currently your only pet?
- What other pets are living in your home?
- Has your pet lived with children *(list ages)*? Is your pet comfortable with children? If not, please explain.
- Has your pet lived with other animals *(list types)*? Is your pet comfortable with other animals? If not, please explain.
- Does your pet live strictly outdoors?
- Does your pet live strictly indoors?
- Does your pet live in and out? Do you have a special door for their use?
- Does your pet live mainly in a garage or porch?
- Is your pet housetrained? Not housetrained? How often do accidents occur?
- As the pet owner, do you have any additional information about your pet's socialization abilities?

Your Pet's Diet & Feeding Schedule

- Does your pet have any food allergies? What type of food (*favorite brand of food, supplements, snacks, etc.*) does your pet like to eat?
- What is your pet's feeding schedule *(a.m./p.m.)*?
- How much food is given at each feeding time?
- What kind/brand of pet food?
- Where is the pet food purchased?
- Where is the pet food stored?
- What are the pet's favorite treats?
- Where is your pet's feeding bowl located?
- Where is your pet's fresh water supply located?
- Does your pet have any food allergies?
- Does your pet take any special medications (*e.g. heartworm medicine and/or flea medicine, etc.*), supplements or have any other special dietary needs?
- As the pet owner, do you have any additional information about your pet's diet to share?

Healthy Pet Food/Nutrition Tips

- Monitor your pet's weight, diet and caloric intake by measuring food and limiting treats
- Avoid human food – it can upset a dog's stomach and diet
- Discuss your pet's diet needs with your veterinarian especially nutritional requirements for age or breed specific food supplements
- Provide fresh, clean water daily

Your Pet's Exercise and Play Schedule

- Does your pet go for regularly scheduled walks in your neighborhood? What time of day do you usually go out?
- What are your pet's favorite places to exercise *(local parks, walking areas, hiking spots, etc.)?*
- What is your pet's favorite exercise activity?
- Does your pet have any phobias or fears *(e.g. skateboards, lawnmowers, bicycles, loud sirens thunder, etc.)?*
- Is your pet comfortable around other dogs/cats? Strangers? Small children? Loud noises? Strange places?
- Where is the pet's collar and leash kept?
- Is your pet trained to walk comfortably without pulling on a leash?
- Do you ever employ a dog walker to provide additional exercise for your pet? If so, how often?
- Does your pet respond to any verbal/non-verbal words/ commands? What are they?
- Does your pet know any special tricks?
- Does your pet like to exercise year around *(also consider the climate, monitor temperatures to determine the best time of day to exercise your pet)?*
- What games does your pet like to play *(favorite toys, Frisbee, etc.)?*
- Do you have any indoor exercise activities that your pet enjoys? Do you have an enclosed and safe backyard/play area?
- How would you rate your pet's social skills?
- What is your pet's favorite way of being petted and/or brushed?
- Is your pet comfortable at a dog park? Are there any parks located near your residence?

- How do you calm your pet down when he or she is upset or nervous?
- Which holidays do you celebrate? Halloween? Christmas? Etc. How does your pet react to parties and/or social events?
- Does your pet have any *'animal friends'* that visit? How often?
- Has your pet ever bitten another dog or been aggressive playing with other animals? In your opinion, what circumstances might cause your pet to bite/scratch?
- Does your pet know how to swim? Do you own a pool?
- Does your pet play well and safely at the beach and/or lake?
- Does your pet go hunting? Has your pet had any additional training for this sport?
- Does your pet perform any tasks/jobs in your home, ranch, farm, etc.?
- Has your pet ever been to an agility park to exercise?
- Has your pet attended obedience training? If so, when and with whom?
- As the pet owner, do you have any additional information about your pet's exercise routine to share?

Pet Exercise Tips

- Exercise your pet regularly, as recommended by your veterinarian
- Select toys that are safe, sturdy and stimulating for your pet, such as hard rubber balls
- Practice safety in the yard, on walks and trips by using barriers, leashes, carriers and proper identification
- Socialize your dog around other pets and people to help him or her learn to adjust to changes his/her environment

Your Pet's Nap/Sleep Schedule

- Does the pet have a routine prior to bedtime and upon awakening?
- What is the pet's normal bedtime/sleep time?
- Where is your pet's usual sleeping area? Do they have a special bed and/or blanket?
- Any unusual circumstances that would keep your pet awake at night?
- What other pets are in your home? Do they sleep with your pet?
- Does your pet sleep strictly outdoors?
- Does your pet sleep strictly indoors?
- Does your pet sleep in and out? Do you have a special door for their use?
- Does your pet sleep mainly in a garage or porch?
- Does your pet sleep in a crate? Where is it located?
- Consider providing your pet with something that has your smell on it *(e.g. scarf, shirt or old sweater* to help your pet adjust and bond with the *Pet Caregiver/Guardian (just in case)*
- As the pet owner, do you have any additional information about your pet's sleeping routine to share?

Your Pet's Grooming Schedule

- Do you have your pet professionally groomed?
- What is the name and location of your pet groomer?
- How often do you have your pet groomed? Which treatments do you choose for your pet during your grooming visit?
- Do you bathe your pet at home? Where? How often?
- Does your pet enjoy being bathed and groomed?

- How does your pet like to be petted and/or brushed?
- What products do you use to care for your pet's fur and skin?
- How often do you brush your pet's fur? Does your pet shed? How do you manage this?
- How often do you clean your pet's ears? Is your pet prone to having ear infections?
- Does your pet have any allergies to grooming products? If so, what?
- Do you brush your pet's teeth? If so, how often? What products do you use?
- Do you trim your pet's nails? If so, how often?
- Do you have a copy of your pet's rabies vaccine on file with your grooming professional?
- As the pet owner, do you have any additional information about your pet's grooming routine to share?

Location of Important Pet Supplies and *Pet Protection Trust* Documents

- Location of your pet's food supply
- Location of your pet's water bowl
- Location of your pet's litter box/potty area?
- Location of your pet's leash and collar?
- Location of your pet's play toys and balls?
- Location of your pet's brush for grooming?
- Location of your pet's bed/crate?
- Location of an extra house key?
- Location of the *Pet First Aid Kit*?
- Location of the *Pet Emergency Preparedness Disaster Supply Kit*?
- Location of a copy of the "*Pet Protection Daily Care Guide™*" and "*Pet Protection Trust*" documents?

IV. Your Pet's Medical Information

Your Pet's Veterinarian:

Name:

Address *(Street, City, State, & Zip Code)*:

Phone:

Email/Website:

Your Pet's Emergency Veterinarian:

Name:

Address *(Street, City, State, & Zip Code)*:

Phone:

Email/Website:

Location of 24-hour Emergency Clinic:

Name:

Address *(Street, City, State, & Zip Code)*:

Phone:

Email/Website:

Your Pet's Annual check up appointment:

Date:

Your Pet's Rabies & Vaccination schedule:

Date:

Your Pet's Other Medical Specialist(s):

Name:

Address *(Street, City, State, & Zip Code)*:

Phone:

Email/Website:

Information on Pet Medical Insurance

Do you own a *Pet Medical Insurance* policy? If not, you may want to consider purchasing one for your pet as no one can predict when a pet may have an accident or develop a chronic condition or life-threatening illness-a pet health insurance plan will help both you and your *Pet Caregiver/Guardian* deal with any unexpected veterinary costs.

Here are some features to consider when choosing a *Pet Medical Insurance* policy for your pet:

- **Find out exactly what procedures are covered:** Learn up front how much the *Pet Medical Insurance Policy* will pay including any deductibles and what will be covered and what won't. Some policies will cover up to 90% of all out-of-pocket veterinary costs with an affordable deductible.

- **How much coverage does your pet need?** Some *Pet Medical Insurance Policies* cover all accidents, illnesses, diagnostic tests, medications, hospital stays and veterinary supplements at any veterinary practice, emergency hospital or specialty facility. Find out exactly what the policy you are considering covers. You may also want to add an additional wellness plan/policy that covers routine care such as dental cleaning, vaccines and flea control medications.

- **Can your pet see any vet at any time, anywhere and still be covered?** Find out if you can go to your own vet, get a second opinion at a different vet clinic and/or go to a specialist hospital or an emergency clinic. Also, if you travel, find out if you can take your pet to any licensed veterinarian in the United States and if the costs will still be covered.

- **What are the cancellation policies of the *Pet Medical Insurance Company*?** Find out if your *Pet Medical Insurance Company* will cancel or decrease your coverage if you have an unlucky or sickly pet.
- **How easy and fast is the claim process?** Find out from the *Pet Medical Insurance Company* how quickly you will receive reimbursement on pet medical claims.

Pet Medical Insurance Information

Agent Name:

Address *(Street, City, State, & Zip Code)*:

Phone:

Email/Website:

Policy number and Insurance Company:

Date of Purchase:

Monthly fee:

Location of Policy:

Your Pet's Medical History

- How would you describe the overall health of your pet?
- Does your pet have any chronic medical conditions to be monitored? If so, what?
- Does your pet have any allergies? If so, how do you help him/her feel better?
- Has your pet had any surgery? If so, for what?
- Are there any special considerations for your pet's breed?
- In general, how long is this breed's life span?
- Are there any illnesses, diseases, etc. that seem to occur more often with your pet's breed?
- What are they?
- Does your pet take any prescription medicine for any condition? If so, what? How often?
- Does your pet take any over the counter supplements for any condition? If so, what? How often?
- Where are your pet's medication/supplements stored?
- Does your pet have any regular flea/tick control treatments? If so, what brand is used? How often?
- Where are all of your pet's medical records, inoculation and spay/neuter certificates, etc., located?
- Where do you keep a schedule/log of vaccinations and medical check-ups?
- Where is your *Pet First Aid Kit* located?
- Where is your *Pet Emergency Preparedness Disaster Supply Kit* located?
- As the *pet owner*, do you have any additional information about your pet's medical history or other health challenges to share?

Please add extra notes to your *"Pet Customized Care Agreement™"* to indicate any special handling that is required for your pet and any additional recommendations for the animal's care *(especially if you have an aging or special needs pet)*. Always keep copies of vaccination and medical records handy. Document any known issues about your pet such as allergic reactions and sensitivities. Remember also to discuss your *Pet Protection Trust* arrangements with your veterinarian. Some vets may want you to complete a *Veterinary Care Contract* or *Authorization Form* to allow for someone else *(e.g. your Pet Caregiver/Guardian)* to consent for your pet's medical care.

Your Pet's Prescription Medicines

Provide any information regarding your pet's prescription and/or supplements or flea/tick/heartworm medicines, etc. below. If your companion pet is taking any prescription medicine for a particular condition, please indicate the information below for each prescription the pet is currently taking:

- Date the medication was prescribed
- Pet's name
- Pet owners name
- Prescribing veterinarian's name
- Address and telephone number of the facility filling the prescription
- Reason the medication is needed
- Amount of medication dispensed (*milliliters, ounces, number of tablets or capsules*)
- Strength of the medication (*milligrams, micrograms*)
- Dosage and duration of treatment

- Route of administration (*orally, applied to the skin, in the ear*)
- Number of refills and expiration date
- Cautionary instructions (*shake well, keep refrigerated, etc.*)

Healthy Preventive Medical Care Tips for Pets

- Plan to maintain regular veterinarian visits for routine health check-ups including vaccinations and preventative care measures
- Find information and learn more about the breed of your dog/cat for any specific diseases or body conditions *(examine coat, ribs, eyes, ears and nose regularly)*
- Grooming regularly by brushing, bathing and clipping according to breed, size and your dog/cat's indoor or outdoor habits
- Always post emergency numbers and keep a pet first-aid kit and supplies close *by (e.g. gauze, bandages, eyewash, tweezers, cold pack, thermometer, towel and gloves)*
- Keep a copy of your pet's *"Advanced Health Care Directive for Pets"* up-to-date and available in case you are unable to be present for a pet's emergency treatment due to illness or disability
- Consider spaying or neutering your pet to help improve a dog/cat's disposition, prevent unwanted behaviors and reduce the chance for infections, tumors and cancers
- Observe your pet daily and look for any change in behavior or eating habits that might signal a medical problem
- Plan to brush your pet's teeth weekly and encourage the pet to chew toys and/or biscuits for additional teeth cleaning
- Plan to keep a log and/or record of all medical check-ups, vaccinations, allergies, etc. to share in the *"Pet Protection Daily Care Guide™"*

Advanced Health Care Directive for Pets

An "*Advanced Health Care Directive for Pets*" (Power of Attorney) names a person, usually the *Pet Caregiver/Guardian* who can step in immediately and take care of your pet if you're alive, but unable or unwilling to act due to an accident, hospitalization, injury, or illness. Completing the "*Advanced Health Care Directive for Pets*" will give the pet owner the peace-of-mind of knowing that your pet is safe. The *Pet Caregiver/Guardian* in conjunction with your veterinarian will then be able to immediately provide the necessary health care and make any critical medical decisions to provide for the welfare of your pet.

When your emergency is over, you can simply rescind the "*Advanced Health Care Directive for Pets*" and return to taking personal care of your pet. It will only be used in case of an emergency and is for the protection of you and your pet.

Advanced Health Care Directive for Pets

In the event of my incapacity to act or death, I would like for the following plan for the care and safety of my Pet to be implemented.

Pet's Name _____ Breed _____

Age _____ Gender _____

I would like for my pet to be placed in the care of the *Pet Caregiver/ Guardian*, as listed below:

Pet Caregiver/Guardian Information
Name:
Address *(Street, City, State, & Zip Code)*:
Phone:
Email:

☐ My appointed *Pet Caregiver/Guardian* has a copy of this document and has a copy of my pet's medical records.

Veterinarian Information
Name:
Address *(Street, City, State, & Zip Code)*:
Phone:
Email/Website:

☐ My Veterinarian has a copy of this document and has a copy of my pet's medical records.

(Pet Owner Signature) _____ (Date) _____
(Witness Signature) _____ (Date) _____
Notary of the Public Seal: _____ (Date) _____

Pet Emergency Preparedness Plan Including a Pet First Aid/Disaster Supply Kit

Pet First Aid Kit

Remember that any first aid that is administered to a pet should be followed by immediate veterinary care. First aid care is not a substitute for veterinary care, but it may save your pet's life until it receives veterinary treatment. When a pet is hurt, it's owner or caregiver needs to get help right away. A *Pet First Aid Kit* will help the pet owner deal with any minor injuries or stabilize a pet on the way to the vet for treatment. Plan to assemble a *Pet First Aid Kit* and have it available in an accessible place, just in case. To avoid the feelings of panic that may accompany these situations, it is recommended that you (or your *Pet Caregiver/Guardian*) take the following steps to get prepared for a potential pet medical emergency. Here is a suggested list of contents for a simple *Pet First Aid Kit (plan to store these items in a waterproof, portable container):*

- *Pet First Aid Book*
- Latex (or hypoallergenic material) gloves
- Gauze sponges (a variety of sizes)
- Gauze rolls, 2-inch width
- Elastic cling bandage
- Material to make a splint
- Adhesive tape, hypoallergenic
- Non-adherent sterile pads
- Small scissors
- Tweezers
- Magnifying glass
- Grooming clippers or safety razor
- Nylon leash
- Towel
- Muzzle
- Compact emergency "blanket" *(available in the camping department of many stores)*
- Water-based sterile lubricant
- Hydrogen peroxide (3%)
- Rubbing alcohol;
- Topical antibiotic ointment
- Antiseptic towelettes
- Insect sting stop pads
- Cotton-tipped swabs
- Instant cold pack
- Epsom salts
- Baby-dose syringe or eyedropper
- Sterile eye lubricant
- Sterile saline wash
- Safety pins *(medium size 4)*
- Tongue depressors
- Diphenhydramine, if approved by your veterinarian
- Glucose paste or syrup
- Styptic powder or pencil
- Plastic card (such as old credit card) to scrape away stingers
- List of emergency phone numbers including those for your pet's veterinarian, and the after hours emergency veterinary hospital
- Petroleum jelly
- Penlight with batteries (AA)
- Clean clothe
- Needle-nose pliers
- Copy of the '*Pet Alert Wallet Card*'
- Copy of '*Home Alert 'In Case of Emergency Card*'
- Your Pet's Medical Information

Here is an example of a *Pet First Aid Kit* that you can easily locate and purchase online or at your local Pet Supply store:

Pet Emergency Preparedness and Disaster Supply Kit *(Additional supplies for an emergency disaster and/or evacuation)*

In addition to being prepared for a medical emergency in your home, it is critical to be prepared for a disaster too. Life is unpredictable, emergencies and natural weather disasters can occur at any time. We just don't know when or where. If you must evacuate your residence whether you are away from home for a day or a week due to an unexpected emergency, you will need essential supplies. The *Red Cross* advises that you may not be home when an evacuation order or emergency occurs. Find out if a trusted neighbor or your *Pet Caregiver/Guardian* would be willing to take your pet and meet you at a prearranged location. This person should be comfortable with your pet, know where your animal is likely to be, know where your *Pet Emergency Preparedness and Disaster Supply Kit* is kept, and have a key to your home. If you use a pet sitting service, they may be available to help, but you need to discuss the possibility with them well in advance.

Disaster may strike, any one of us, at any time. We just don't know when or where. As a pet owner, you have the responsibility of planning for your pet's care during any unpredictable chaotic emergency. According the *American Red Cross*, the best way to protect your family (*and your pet companions*) from the effects of a disaster is to have a disaster plan in place. Being prepared can save their lives. Different disasters require different responses. But whether the disaster is an earthquake, flood, hurricane or a hazardous spill, you may have to evacuate your home.

Planning and preparation for an emergency now will enable you to evacuate with your pet quickly and safely. But keep in mind that animals, both cats and dogs, react differently under stress. Outside your home and in the car, keep dogs securely leashed and transport cats in carriers. Don't leave animals unattended anywhere as they can easily run off. Even the calmest pet may panic, hide, and try to escape, or even bite or scratch during an emergency situation. And, when you return home, give your pet time to settle back into their routines.

If you find yourself with an impending weather emergency, you need to have a plan in place to protect your pets. The *U.S. Department of Homeland Security's Federal Emergency Management Agency (FEMA)* has some suggestion to help: "The family pet can be overlooked until the final frantic moments before a resident evacuates, but a little planning can ensure pet safety and care during an such an emergency. Taking the pet along is the most important thing individuals or families can do for their animals during any type of weather emergency evacuation. Pets that are left behind can be injured, lost or killed during a hurricane, earthquake, flood, etc. Pet owners should put an emergency evacuation disaster plan in place for animals before an emergency threatens your safety. Evacuation preparation is a key focus of the *"Stay Alert: Stay Alive"* National

Emergency Preparedness campaign. Just like with your family, evacuation plans for animals take time to plan and execute properly. The most important thing you can do for your pet now is to make sure their immunizations are current and they have proper identification. Remember, many emergency shelters do not allow pets, except for service animals, so it is important to identify in advance those that do in your area."

Until a very short time ago, pets were not allowed in most emergency shelters and were not eligible for rescue with their owners. Many of us watched in horror as the people in hurricane stricken New Orleans sat helpless in their homes and on their roofs refusing to be rescued without their pets. Statistics have shown that many more people and animals could have been saved at that time if pets had been eligible for rescue along with their owners. *The Pet Evacuation and Transportation Standards (PETS) Act* was signed into law in October of 2006. This Federal Law has changed now and it allows pets to be evacuated along with their owners in the event of an emergency. Some of the other provisions of the *PETS Act* include:

- Local and state emergency preparedness authorities must include plans for pets and service animals in disaster plans to qualify for *FEMA* grants.
- *FEMA* is authorized to assist state and local communities in developing disaster plans that include pets and service animals and Federal funds may be used to create pet-friendly emergency shelters and to provide assistance to families with pets and the pets themselves following major disasters.
- Special facilities have been created for families with pets and/or foster homes for pets of displaced families by *FEMA, Red Cross, Humane Society* and other

organizations. Check online for details in your county. Often, disaster evacuation warnings are issued with very short notice—at the first hint of disaster, act to protect your pet. Plan ahead to insure that both you, your family and companion pet will have a safe place to stay. In addition to your original *Pet First Aid Kit* you may want to assemble these additional items in case you must vacate your residence due to a disaster. If you live in an area with severe weather conditions, etc., you may want to take an old suitcase and fill it with the emergency supplies listed below and keep it either in your car or near your front door exit for quick access.

Your *Pet Emergency Preparedness and Disaster Supply Kit* should include the following items:

- Include a sturdy leash, collar, ID, harnesses, and/or carriers to transport pet safely and ensure that your animals can't escape
- Include a copy of your *"Pet Protection Legal Care Plan"* (which includes the information on your pet's feeding schedule, medical conditions, and behavior problems, etc.)
- Include a supply of food, portable water supply, bowls, cat litter/pan, and a can opener
- Include blankets and/or a pet bed and toys, if easily transportable
- Include a current photo of your pet in case they get lost
- Include the *Pet First Aid Kit* (including any medications stored in waterproof containers)

Be ready ahead-of-time by contacting a list of hotels, motels, boarding facilities and veterinarians who could shelter your pet in case of an emergency; include the 24-hour contact phone numbers). Call ahead to reserve and confirm the emergency shelter arrangements you have made for you and your pet. Plan ahead now and do the research now to locate a safe out-of-the-area shelter for both you and your pet.

Health Care Tips for Your Pet

Tips to Help You Understand Your Companion Pet's Distress/Pain Symptoms

Dogs: Is your dog in pain? Dogs' responses to pain vary. Some dogs are very stoic, and will show few outward signs even when in extreme pain. Others are more dramatic, and will make their pain quite clear. A dog in pain may:

- Pant
- Limp, favor a painful area, or resent it when a painful area is touched
- Acts agitated or refuse to lie down, rest, or sleep
- Become aggressive or suffer personality changes
- Loses its appetite and hide/act withdrawn
- Whine, whimper, or vocalize *(this occurs less often in cats)*.
- Stand with its back arched

Cats: Is your cat in pain? Cats' instinctively hide pain. Therefore, signs of pain in a cat are usually very subtle. A cat in pain may:

- Limp, favor a painful area, or resent it when a painful area is touched
- Hide or act quiet and withdrawn
- Lose its appetite
- Breathe rapidly or pant

- Act agitated or refuses to lie down, rest, or sleep
- Become aggressive or suffer personality changes
- Vocalization *(howling or crying)* may be a sign of anxiety, agitation, fear, hunger, or severe pain
- Most cats suffering from pain do not vocalize. Lack of vocalization should not be construed as absence of pain

Tips to Help Keep Your Companion Pet Cool in Hot Weather

- The normal body temperature for a dog is 101 to 102 degrees
- A 3-degree rise can put a dog into a dangerous situation and increase its need for oxygen
- At 108 degrees the heart, brain, liver, kidneys, and intestinal tracts begin to break down
- If the pavement or sidewalk is too hot for your feet, it's too hot for your dog's paws *(the pads can easily be burned on hot days)*
- Never ever leave your dog or cat in a car
- If you let your pet outside, make sure that they have plenty of water available and provide him or her with access to a shady spot, a sprinkler, wading pool, and/or sand pit soaked with water
- If you believe that your pet is overheating bring it into air conditioning immediately
- You can immerse it in cool *(not cold)* water and give it "sips" of water. If necessary, apply ice packs and immediately take your dog or cat to your veterinarian

Tips to Help Keep Your Companion Pet Safe from Household Poisons

- Dogs that watch you plant bulbs may dig them up and many types of bulbs can be poisonous *(store pesticides and fertilizers out of reach of pets)*
- Make sure that pets are not sniffing grass seed into their noses
- Keep pets away from hot barbeque grills or coals
- Keep your dog or cat away from lighter fluid, insect repellant, glow in the dark jewelry, and sunscreen—all of these items are potentially lethal if inhaled or ingested
- Keep dogs and cats away from picnic foods such as alcoholic beverages, chocolate and other foods like onions, grapes, raisins, avocado, and coffee—all of which can be toxic to pets
- Keep pets away from Styrofoam and plastic utensils used at picnics and parties and the plastic wrap and strings that cover raw meat *(these items are alluring to pets and will lead to gastrointestinal obstruction when ingested, which may require surgery)*
- Dogs or cats with white noses or ear tips can sunburn easily *(it is best to keep the pet in the shade)*

V. Contact List: Pet Care Support Advisors

Pet Owner and Emergency Contact Information

Name of Pet Owner

Name:
Address *(Street, City, State, & Zip Code)*:
Phone:
Email:
Pet Name:

Name of Closest Neighbor

Name:
Address *(Street, City, State, & Zip Code)*:
Phone:
Email:

Name of Closest Family Member Living Nearby

Name:
Address *(Street, City, State, & Zip Code)*:
Phone:
Email:

Pet Caregiver/Guardian Contact Information

Name of Pet Caregiver/Guardian

Name:
Address *(Street, City, State, & Zip Code)*:
Phone:
Email:

Pet Caregiver/Guardian (back-up)

Name:
Address *(Street, City, State, & Zip Code)*:
Phone:
Email:

Pet Financial Caregiver/Trustee Contact Information

Name of Pet Financial Caregiver/Trustee

Name:
Address *(Street, City, State, & Zip Code)*:
Phone:
Email:

Name of Pet Financial Caregiver/Trustee (back-up)

Name:
Address *(Street, City, State, & Zip Code)*:
Phone:
Email:

Pet Financial Assets (Monetary Funds) Information and List of Advisors

Your Pet's Bank Account (funds to be managed by the Pet Financial Caregiver/Trustee)

Bank Manager's Name:
Address *(Street, City, State, & Zip Code)*:
Phone:
Bank account number:
Email/Website:

Your "Pet Protection Trust" and Family Estate Planning Attorney

Attorney's Name:
Firm Address *(Street, City, State, & Zip Code)*:
Phone:
Email/Website:

Pet Medical Information and List of Advisors

Your Pet's Veterinarian

Veterinarian's Name:
Address *(Street, City, State, & Zip Code)*:
Phone:
Email/Website:

Your Pet's Emergency Clinic Information (opens 24/7)

Name:
Address *(Street, City, State, & Zip Code)*:
Phone:
Email/Website:

Animal Poison Control Center Information

(888-426-4435)

Pet Insurance Information and List of Advisors

Pet Medical Insurance Information

Agent Name:
Address *(Street, City, State, & Zip Code)*:
Phone:
Email/Website:
Policy number and Insurance Company:
Date of Purchase:
Monthly fee *(include information on deductibles, co-pays, maximum payouts, waiting periods, coverage for pre-existing conditions)*:
Location of Policy:

Pet Liability Insurance Information

Agent Name:
Address *(Street, City, State, & Zip Code)*:
Phone:
Email/Website:
Policy number and Insurance Company:
Date of Purchase:
Monthly fee:
Location of Policy:

Pet Life Insurance Information

Agent Name:
Address *(Street, City, State, & Zip Code)*:
Phone:
Email/Website:
Policy number and Insurance Company:
Date of Purchase:
Monthly fee:
Location of Policy:

Pet _____ *Insurance-Information*

Agent Name:
Address *(Street, City, State, & Zip Code)*:
Phone:
Email/Website:
Policy number and Insurance Company:
Date of Purchase:
Monthly fee:
Location of Policy:

Miscellaneous Pet Information and List of Advisors (e.g. Groomers, Boarding Facilities, etc.)

Your Pet Boarding Facility/Day Care Center

Name:
Address *(Street, City, State & Zip Code)*:
Phone:
Email/Website:

Your Pet Sitter

Name:
Address *(Street, City, State & Zip Code)*:
Phone:
Email/Website:

Your Dog Walker

Name:
Address *(Street, City, State & Zip Code)*
Phone:
Email/Website:

Your Pet's "Pals" (other animals that your animal plays with or walks with)

Name:

Address *(Street, City, State & Zip Code)*:

Phone:

Email:

Your Pet's Groomer

Name:

Address *(Street, City, State & Zip Code)*:

Phone:

Email/Website:

Your Pet's Trainer/Behaviorist

Name:

Address *(Street, City, State & Zip Code)*:

Phone:

Email/Website:

Your Pet's AKC- Pet Handler, Breeder, Show Contacts, etc.

Name:

Address *(Street, City, State & Zip Code)*:

Phone:

Email/Website:

Pet Breeder/ Pet Family-of-Origin

Name:

Address *(Street, City, State & Zip Code)*:

Phone:

Email/Website:

Your Pet's Food Store

Name:
Address *(Street, City, State & Zip Code)*:
Phone:
Email/Website:

Your Pet's Hospice

Name:
Address *(Street, City, State & Zip Code)*:
Phone:
Email/Website:

Your Choice of Pet Cemetery

Name:
Address *(Street, City, State & Zip Code)*:
Phone:
Email/Website:

Your Other Pet Advisor(s)

Name:
Address *(Street, City, State & Zip Code)*:
Phone:
Email/Website:

VI. Your Pet's End-of-Life Plan Including Care Instructions for an Aging Pet

As your pet grows older, sometimes there are extenuating circumstances that make it difficult to keep your pet in the care of a non-professional (i.e. the *Pet Caregiver/Guardian*). There are now special organizations with trained medical professionals that offer end-of-life care for your pet, including pet retirement homes and hospice care. What would you like your *Pet Caregiver/Guardian* to do if your pet becomes seriously ill? Pet end-of-life health care choices can be a challenging to resolve.

Because medical treatments for pets are expanding, many of the decisions around life support measures and continuing medical care need to be addressed in your *Pet Protection Trust*. The pet industry has grown exponentially and continues to offer new pet cancer treatments and joint replacement procedures, pet hospice care, pet cemeteries etc. Take the time now to think about your thoughts and recommendations regarding your pet's end-of-life care. Share your thoughts and give some direction now to your *Pet Caregiver/ Guardian* and *Pet Financial Caregiver/Trustee* to guide them during an often sad and difficult time. In addition, you need to discuss and document your wishes regarding the final disposition of your pet and the set of circumstances in which euthanasia would be permitted.

As the *Pet Owner* you may also want to request that your *Family Estate Planning Attorney* to include a statement in your estate plan "that if you are required due to medical issues, etc. to move into an assisted living facilitythat permits your pet to stay with you." You want to have your *Family Estate Planning Attorney* review your *"Pet Protection Trust"* documents and add it to your other estate planning documents.

Pet Hospice Information and End-of-Life Health Care Choices

Hospice care has now expanded to include pets, consider reviewing the available resources in your community with your veterinarian. Probably the most highly regarded program for hospice care for pets is the *Nikki Hospice Foundation for Pets*. With its corporate headquarters in California, this non-profit organization has a wealth of information and guidelines regarding hospice care for animals. The *Foundation* is dedicated to providing veterinary hospice care to terminally ill and dying pets in the comfort of their own homes and subscribes to a philosophy that is very similar to the human hospice programs—the physical, emotional and spiritual needs of these pets and of the people who love them is their first priority. According to their guidelines, "the use of veterinary hospice care is to be considered as constituting good veterinary medicine in that it allows for a "good death" for the pet and consequently, "good" grieving for the client. This service must be offered in the context of a valid veterinarian/client/patient relationship, and it is recommended that appropriate client consent be obtained for all facets of veterinary hospice care."

Making arrangements for your pet's end-of-life care plan can be a challenging process to discuss with your *Pet Caregiver/Guardian* and *Pet Financial Caregiver/Trustee*. Every year there are huge leaps in medical treatments for pets and as a result the decisions and difficult choices around life support measures and continuing medical care need to be addressed by you in your *Pet Protection Trust*. The pet industry has grown exponentially and continues to develop and offer new medical treatments including pet cancer research and joint replacement procedures, pet hospice care, etc. Take time now to think about your recommendations regarding your own pet's end-of-life care and communicate your decisions to your *Pet Caregiver/Guardian* to guide them during a potentially sad and difficult time. In addition, you need to decide how the final disposition of your pet's remains will be handled too.

As the *Pet Owner* you need to discuss with your *Pet Caregiver/ Guardian* to what extent you would support extraordinary measures to keep your pet alive. Plan to also discuss with both of your pet's caregivers the circumstances in which you would consider euthanasia for your pet's comfort and welfare. For instance, if your pet needs open heart surgery to keep his or her heart beating, do you want the veterinarian to proceed with such an invasive procedure? Pets may not be euthanized unless their quality of life is compromised. veterinarians must follow the law that only allows an animal to be euthanized for reasons of health and/or quality of life. Under what circumstances would you consider euthanasia for your pet? In the event your pet dies, do you want an autopsy?

Tips on Planning Your Pet's Funeral and Final Disposition

Information on a Pet Cemetery Burial

When your pet passes away one day, your *Pet Caregiver/Guardian* will need to have your direction on how you would like to honor your pet's life. There are many services available now that allow for cremation and/or other burial arrangements. Cremation is a less expensive option, than the burial option, just as it is for humans. However, more and more people are putting their pets' remains in special pet cemeteries. There are now many cemeteries in our country that are specifically designed for companion pet remains. Most people ask their veterinarian to take care of disposing of their pet's remains including cremation, a choice of urns and various other offerings.

Over the years, it has become much easier to locate a pet cemetery for the remains of your pet. In fact, there are now pet cemeteries in nearly every state; some have literally dozens. For many pet owners, a formal cemetery burial seems a more fitting tribute to their beloved pet. Burial in a pet cemetery also ensures that your pet's remains will be undisturbed, and cared for *"in perpetuity"*. A cemetery burial can be a costly option, but many families find it a comforting, secure way to handle a pet's remains. A pet cemetery will usually be able to pick up your *Pet Caregiver/Guardian's* home or from the veterinarian's office. If you wish, you can make arrangements for a complete funeral and memorial service too by documenting exactly what kind of program you would like your *Pet Caregiver/Guardian* to provide for your pet.

Many pet owners feel that providing a dignified burial or cremation for their beloved companion pet is a final, fitting act of farewell. They feel that it is the last act of love that they can offer a pet, and it is an important act of closure. Once again it is critical to convey your thoughts and wishes to both your *Pet Caregiver/Guardian* and the *Pet Financial Caregiver/Trustee*. Do you want your pet to be buried or cremated? Do you have a cemetery plot reserved for your pet? If so, where? Do you want to have a funeral/celebration of life ceremony for your pet? If so, where? Do you want to have a funeral/celebration of life ceremony for your pet? If so, please describe the schedule of activities in detail.

Information on Pet Cremation

If you choose to keep your pet's remains with you, it is recommended that you consider having your pet's remains cremated and returned to the *Pet Caregiver/Guardian*. Many veterinarians offer services that provide cremation and then the pet's ashes are placed in a decorative urn or container. Pet crematories can now be found in many cities; a pet crematory can usually pick up your pet's remains from your veterinarian or from the *Pet Caregiver/Guardian's* home. Other choices include scattering a pet's ashes rather than preserving them. Some pet owners choose to have their pet's ashes scattered in the pet's own yard, where it has lived and played (this is another way of bringing the pet "home" one last time). Others choose to have their pet's ashes scattered in a way that symbolizes setting the pet "free" for its final journey—such as in the woods or over a body of water, or just into the wind.

How to Create a Philanthropic Legacy to Honor Your Pet's Life

Terminating the "Pet Trust" and Making the Financial Distribution to the Beneficiaries

Upon the passing of your pet, if there are any funds still available in the *"Pet Protection Trust"*, for your pet's care, you need to indicate how you would like these remaining funds to be distributed. As the *Pet Owner* you may want to consider leaving the funds to the *Pet Caregiver/Guardian, Pet Financial Caregiver/Trustee, Pet Hospice* or another organization that you would choose to support. Your choice is your philanthropic legacy in honor of your pet. If you want to choose several beneficiaries, most *Family Estate Planning Attorneys* recommend that you indicate a percentage of remaining funds instead of a dollar amount.

Information on Pet Grief, Pet Loss and Bereavement Resources

Pet's Grieve the Loss of Their Owner

If you pass away first, your pet will grieve for you. More and more research is showing how companion pets are able to understand human emotion, sadness, joy and grief. Your pet will go through a difficult time learning to adjust to their new 'family'. Ideally your designated *Pet Caregiver/Guardian* will do everything possible to make this transition easier for your pet. It is important to keep as many familiar activities as possible including meals, walks, etc. Sometimes providing a piece of your clothing *(like a t-shirt)* to the care provider will provide comfort during the time of transition to a new home.

Moving Through the Grief Over the Loss of a Pet

When either a pet owner or the *Pet Caregiver/Guardian* goes through a pet's passing, coping with the death of a pet can be very challenging. Since our pet's have much shorter life spans than humans, most likely you and your family will have to go through this difficult process one day. Both the *Pet Caregiver/Guardian* and the *Pet Financial Caregiver/ Trustee* might benefit from the recommendations and resources listed below. Many forms of support are available now for grieving pet owners and caregivers including pet bereavement counseling services, pet loss support hotlines, and local or online bereavement groups, books, videos, and magazine articles. Here are a few suggestions to help pet owners and caregivers cope with the loss of a pet:

- Be gentle with yourself and try not to judge your feelings, most pet owners and caregivers consider their pet to be just like a family member
- Acknowledge the grief and give yourself permission to express it
- Reach out for help and call the *Humane Society* to see whether it offers a pet loss support group or if they could refer you to one
- Consult with your pet's veterinarian about available local pet loss resources

- Go online and look for pet loss support groups and other coping information

When the sad time arrives that your pet does pass away, please be sure to take advantage of all the pet grief support resources available to you, your family members and the caregiver's you have chosen to watch over your beloved pet. When you've established a *Pet Protection Trust* for your pet, you will have taken all of the important steps necessary to ensure the ongoing care of your companion pet in case you become incapacitated or worse. Without such a plan, the fate of your dog or cat is at best uncertain, and at worst, unspeakable.

VII. *Pet Caregiver/Guardian* and *Pet Financial Caregiver/Trustee Agreement* and Acknowledgement of the *"Pet Protection Daily Care Guide™"*:

The parties hereto have read and executed this Agreement this ____ day of _____, 20____.

Signature _____ Date: _____
(FULL NAME), Pet Owner *(Trustor)*

_____ Date: _____
(FULL NAME of Pet)

Signature _____ Date: _____
(FULL NAME) *Pet Caregiver/Guardian*

Signature _____ Date: _____
(FULL NAME) *Pet Caregiver/Guardian (back-up)*

Signature _____ Date: _____
(FULL NAME) *Pet Financial Caregiver/Trustee*

Signature _____ Date: _____
(FULL NAME) *Pet Financial Caregiver/Trustee (back-up)*

Chapter 5

How to Complete the
"Pet Protection Trust"

"Many people have heard the remarkable example of devotion
involving a Skye terrier dog that worked for a Scottish shepherd
named Old Jock. In 1858, the day after Jock was buried
*(with almost nobody present to mourn him except his shaggy
dog)* in the churchyard at *Greyfriars Abbey* in Edinburgh,
Bobby was found sleeping on his master's grave, where he
continued to sleep every night for fourteen years."

~Jeffrey Moussaieff Masson

Finally, you have arrived at the last chapter of the book! One of my
primary goals in writing this book was to avoid the complicated
legalese or "legal language" that is often associated with the estate
planning process. This chapter provides an introduction and
overview of the legal provisions (California laws) that promote the
protection of our companion pets. This chapter includes an example
of a completed *"Pet Protection Trust"* for a dog named, *"Sparky"*
and a blank template for you to use to complete your own pet trust
document. We also offer a more accessible blank *Pet Protection
Trust* template online as on-demand, immediately downloadable

document—visit *www.PetProtectionLegalCarePlan.com* to purchase these forms.

This chapter includes the following information:

1. An introduction and overview of the legal process of completing the *"Pet Protection Trust"*

2. An article entitled, *"10 Reasons to Establish a Pet Protection Trust"* by Francis Burton Doyle, Esq., *Family Estate Planning Attorney*

3. A Copy of *California Probate Code §15212*. (this information is a summary of the current laws in the state of California regarding the creation and legality of a *"Pet Protection Trust"*).

4. Remember to consult with your own *Family Estate Planning Attorney* regarding the current laws in the state which you reside

5. An example of a *"Pet Protection Trust"* for a dog named "Sparky".

6. A copy of a blank template to use to complete your own *"Pet Protection Trust"*

7. Information on how to locate a *Notary of the Public* and get your *"Pet Protection Trust"* documents notarized

8. Information on how to access an online copy of the *"Pet Protection Daily Care Guide™"* and the *"Pet Protection Trust"* document

I. Introduction and Overview of the Process to Complete a *"Pet Protection Trust"*

When the pet owner creates a *"Pet Protection Trust"* the document allows you to specify a sum of money to be used for your pet's continued care and to name both "caregiver/trustees" (*Pet Caregiver/ Guardian* and *Pet Financial Caregiver/Trustee*) to carry out your wishes. Until recently pet trusts in California were "honorary" and could not be legally enforced. Now that ruling has changed and the Probate Code section dealing with pet trusts, Section §15212, has been amended to govern trusts for the care of any animal, defined as *"a domestic or pet animal for the benefit of which a trust has been established."* The trust is enforceable by a person designated in the trust or by a person appointed by the court, or by any person interested in the welfare of the animal or any nonprofit charity that is involved with animal welfare.

Ideally, if you haven't completed your own estate plan this would be an excellent time to create provisions for your pet and protect your other assets too. Making plans for the care of your beloved companion pet is just one aspect of preparing a complete estate plan. A 'proper' estate plan really boils down to documenting your "stuff" *(assets),* your wishes regarding protection of your family, children *(and pets),* your own care *(in case of being incapacitated)* and sharing your legacy and last wishes about end-of-life choices and plans. Remember, the size of your estate is immaterial; your desire to provide a comprehensive estate plan and legacy for your family, yourself and your pet is paramount.

Remember that this pet trust template has been designed and executed in the State of California. Both authors highly recommend that you meet with your own *Family Estate Planning Attorney* to review your

"Pet Protection Trust" and *"Pet Protection Daily Care Guide*™*"* and complete or update your own estate plan. Consult a *Family Estate Planning Attorney* to review your completed *"Pet Protection Trust"* documents, as state laws on pet trusts may differ. Remember that this *Pet Protection Trust* template has been designed and executed in the State of California. If you are using the template in a different state then you may want to review the laws regarding pet trusts in your state. Once again, we highly recommend that you take the completed documents to your attorney, including the *"Pet Protection Daily Care Guide*™*"* and the notarized *"Pet Protection Trust"*, to be reviewed and attached to your current estate plan.

In conclusion, there are three things that can change with regard to your *"Pet Protection Legal Care Plan"*,

1. The circumstances of your life *(Pet Owner)*, your *Pet Caregiver/ Guardian* and/or the *Pet Financial Caregiver/ Trustee* could change such as relocating, health concerns, changes in finances, etc.,

2. The law in your state could be updated/changed and/or

3. You may decide to change the terms of who you want to provide a home for your pet and/or to whom you choose to disperse your assets (financial funds). By reviewing your *"Pet Protection Daily Care Guide*™*"* and the *"Pet Protection Trust"* frequently, you can be sure that your wishes will be carried out, and your companion pet will receive the quality of lifetime care that you want them to have.

Unlike a simple directive in a will, a *"Pet Protection Trust"* provides a host of additional protections and advantages, such as:

- The *"Pet Protection Daily Care Guide™"* and *"Pet Protection Trust"* are valid during the pet owner's life and after his or her death.

- The *"Pet Protection Trust"* can help preempt problems with substantial complicated and involved estates.

- The *"Pet Protection Trust"* is particularly useful if the pet owner expects a contest to the estate *(for example, if the amount left for the pet's care is enough that someone will contest the pet owners mental capacity, or if there is a litigious family member whom the pet owner believes may dispute the final documents).*

- A *"Pet Protection Daily Care Guide™"* and *"Pet Protection Trust"* control the disbursement of funds.

- The *"Pet Protection Trust"* allows provisions for incapacity of the pet owner.

- The *"Pet Protection Daily Care Guide™"* can be completed with or without a lawyer's help. However, we recommended meeting with your *Family Estate Planning Attorney* to add this document to your current estate plan. Any trusted advisor *(such as an accountant, trustee, insurance representative, investment advisor, lawyer, or paralegal)* can help a pet owner/client complete the *"Pet Protection Trust"*.

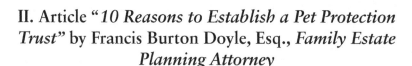

II. Article *"10 Reasons to Establish a Pet Protection Trust"* by Francis Burton Doyle, Esq., *Family Estate Planning Attorney*

For individuals who wish to adequately provide for their beloved pets in the event of their death or disability, a *Pet Protection Trust* (*"Pet Protection Legal Care Plan"*) is the best method to ensure that their wishes will be carried out in a legally proper and effective way. After considering a number of alternative methods *(wills, agreements, durable powers of attorney)* for making provision for one's pet animal in the event of the pet owner's death or disability, the *Pet Protection Trust* (*"Pet Protection Legal Care Plan"*) is the superior choice. Here are ten reasons why:

1. The *Pet Protection Trust* (*"Pet Protection Legal Care Plan"*) is legally sanctioned by a specific statute.

    Unlike alternative methods such provisions in a durable power of attorney or in a pet protection "agreement", *California Probate Code* §15212 expressly authorizes a *Pet Protection Trust* (*"Pet Protection Legal Care Plan"*) and sets forth the specific requirements for establishing one. Authority in a durable power of attorney remains discretionary with the designated attorney in fact who may unilaterally decide not to exercise the power to provide for pets.

    In addition, the authority of an attorney in fact acting under a power of attorney ceases at death. Most so called *"agreements"* with family or friends to provide for pets are not enforceable because in most cases they lack consideration. In contrast, the *Pet Protection Trust* (*"Pet Protection Legal Care Plan")* is legally valid and enforceable by statute. Provisions in a will directing for the care and maintenance of a pet require that the will be probated and this is a very costly and cumbersome alternative.

2. **The *Pet Protection Trust ("Pet Protection Legal Care Plan")* promotes proper funding.**

A *Pet Protection Trust ("Pet Protection Legal Care Plan")* transforms a wish to provide for one's pet in the event of death or disability into a reality. The client determines how much to set aside for the pets care and then commits specific assets to accomplish the task. So long as the pet owner is alive and competent, the owner for any reason can withdraw the funds in the trust. However, in the event of the pet owner's death or disability, the care of the pet is independently funded which reduces the risk that the administrators of the pet owner's estate or his or her attorney in fact can arbitrarily decide that the care of your pet can't be funded because of the needs of creditors and other beneficiaries.

3. **The *Pet Protection Trust ("Pet Protection Legal Care Plan")* is fully revocable and amendable by the Pet Owner during their lifetime.**

During your lifetime the pet owner can revoke or change the trust or withdraw all of the money or other assets in trust. As long as the pet owner is alive and competent, he or she has full power and authority over the funds in the trust. Only in the event of the pet owner's death or incapacity does the trust operate so as to provide funds for the care of the pet.

Further, the pet owner can amend or completely change the trust at any time. From a tax point of view, the pet owner is treated as the owner of the trust and all of its assets so that establishing a *Pet Protection Trust* has absolutely no tax consequence whatsoever. The pet owner's retention of full control over the funds in trust is a very important feature of the *Pet Protection Trust ("Pet Protection Legal Care Plan")*.

4. **The *Pet Protection Trust* (*"Pet Protection Legal Care Plan"*) avoids probate.**

   If the pet owner disposes of their estate by will, the will must be subject to probate. This is particularly true if the will makes a provision for a pet. This causes unnecessary expense and delay in effecting the wishes of the pet owner to provide for the care and maintenance of the companion pet in the event of the pet owners death.

5. **The *Pet Protection Trust* (*"Pet Protection Legal Care Plan"*) is administered separately from the rest of the pet owner's estate.**

   The separate and independent administration of the *Pet Protection Trust ("Pet Protection Legal Care Plan")* apart from the pet owner's other assets and financial affairs is one of its most important features. If the provision for the care and maintenance of the pet is wrapped up with the administration of the pet owner's other assets, delays and complications will arise which will jeopardize the care of the pet. For example, if provision for the pet's care is part of the pet owner's general testamentary plan issues pertaining to the estate's creditors and the other beneficiaries will hamper the ability to provide funding for the care of the pet. With a separate and independent *Pet Protection Trust ("Pet*

Protection Legal Care Plan"), the funding for the needs of the pet will be immediate upon the death or incapacity of the pet owner.

6. **The pet will be provided for in the event of incapacity.**

    In the event the pet owner suffers incapacity, the *Pet Protection Trust ("Pet Protection Legal Care Plan")* provides that the pet receives immediate care and maintenance using the assets of the *Pet Protection Trust ("Pet Protection Legal Care Plan")*. There is no delay in funding and there is no need to obtain court authority through a conservatorship to provide the funding of the pet's care and maintenance. In addition, the attorney-in-fact under the durable power of attorney does not have to determine how to fund the payments for the pet's care because the pet owner has already done that through the *Pet Protection Trust ("Pet Protection Legal Care Plan")*.

7. **The pet will be provided for in the event of death.**

    As explained above, the probate and estate administration of a decedent's assets necessarily involves delay and expense. This is true even if the post mortem administration is conducted through a living trust. Because it is a separate and independent entity, the *Pet Protection Trust ("Pet Protection Legal Care Plan")* allows for the immediate funding of the pet's care and maintenance.

8. **The *Pet Protection Trust* (*"Pet Protection Legal Care Plan"*) provides an opportunity to clearly articulate wishes regarding the specific nature of the pet's care.**

Because of its independent stature, the *Pet Protection Trust* (*"Pet Protection Legal Care Plan"*) allows for a more intense approach to clearly articulating the pet owner's wishes regarding the care of the pet. Provisions in will, other trusts and durable powers of attorney tend to be general and perfunctory. In contrast, because of its focus, the *Pet Protection Trust* (*"Pet Protection Legal Care Plan"*) gives the pet owner a greater opportunity to clearly articulate his or her wishes regarding the care of the pet with particularity. For example, if a pet owner desires a special diet, deliberate grooming schedule, or care at a local boarding facility, these specific items can be set forth right in the trust document (*"Pet Protection Daily Care Guide™"*).

9. **The *Pet Protection Trust* (*"Pet Protection Legal Care Plan"*) provides a system of checks and balances to secure the care of the pet.**

There are many horror stories where funds set aside for the maintenance of a pet are absconded after the death or disability of the pet owner. *California Probate Code* §15212 was amended to prevent such abuse. The trustee is required to account to the beneficiaries who are to receive the balance of the funds after the death of the pet. If the trustee is abusing the funds and not providing for the pet, then the matter can be brought to the attention of the Superior Court for an appropriate remedy. Further, the pet owner can include special provisions in the trust to further the proper use of the funds for the benefit of the pet. For example, the trustee (*"Pet Financial Caregiver/Trustee"*) can be a different person from the one that is actually caring for the pet (*"Pet Caregiver/Guardian"*).

In this scenario, the pet caregiver *("Pet Caregiver/Guardian")* must verify the expenses being incurred for the pet's care to the trustee *("Pet Financial Caregiver/Trustee")* of the *Pet Protection Trust ("Pet Protection Legal Care Plan")*.

10. **The *Pet Protection Trust ("Pet Protection Legal Care Plan")* allows the pet owner to accomplish the dual purpose of providing for the pet's care as well as other intended beneficiaries.**

Many pet owners have the specific goal of providing for the care of their companion pet as well as other beneficiaries *(typically, family members)*. The *Pet Protection Trust ("Pet Protection Legal Care Plan")* allows the pet owner to accomplish this goal by having a specific provision which directs that the pet be cared for during the pet's lifetime and then upon the death of the pet, the directions provide for an easy and efficient disposition of the remaining funds to the remaining beneficiaries.

III. The Laws (Legal Provisions) that Protect Your Companion Pet:

California Probate Code §15212 (*"Pet Protection Legal Care Plan"*)

In brief: The information below is a summary of the law in the state of California regarding the creation and legality of a *"Pet Protection*

Trust". Each state may have different provisions regarding a *"Pet Protection Trust"*. Both authors highly recommend that you meet with your own *Family Estate Planning Attorney* to review your *"Pet Protection Trust"* document and/or complete your own estate plan.

California Cal Probate Code §15212 Year of Enactment: 2008

Summary of law: A trust may be created for the care of an animal or animals alive during the settlor's lifetime. Unless the trust instrument provides otherwise, the trust terminates upon the death of the animal, or upon the death of the last surviving animal covered by the trust.

In full: *California Probate Code;* Trusts for care of animal's duration; requirements; accountings; beneficiaries. A person can create a trust for the care of a domestic or pet animal for the life of the animal. The trust will endure only for the life of the animal. The trust will endure only for the life of the pet, even if the trust contemplates a longer duration. Note that the statute uses the singular form animal and the term domestic pet.

CHAPTER 168

An act to repeal and add Section §15212 of the *California Probate Code*, relating to pet trusts. *[Approved by Governor July 22, 2008. Filed with Secretary of State July 22, 2008.]* Legislative counsels digest SB 685, Yee. Pet trusts. Existing law provides that a trust for the care of a designated domestic or pet animal may be performed by the trustee for the life of the animal, whether or not there is a beneficiary who can seek enforcement or termination of the trust and whether or not the terms of the trust contemplate a longer duration.

This bill would repeal the provisions regarding domestic or pet animal trusts and would provide instead that a trust for the care of a domestic or pet animal is for a lawful non-charitable purpose and terminates when no animal is living on the date of the settlor's death, unless otherwise provided in the trust. The bill would require a court to liberally construe an animal trust to bring it within the bill's provisions, to presume against an interpretation that would render the disposition a mere request or an attempt to honor the animal, and to carry out the general intent of the trust. The bill would provide an order of disposition of trust property upon termination of the trust and would provide authority for the court to name a trustee and to transfer trust property, as specified. This bill would permit any person interested in the welfare of the animal or any nonprofit charitable organization that has as its principal activity the care of animals to petition the court regarding the trust, as specified. The bill would provide a process for an accounting of the trust, to be waived if the value of the trust assets does not exceed $40,000, as specified. The bill would permit beneficiaries of the trust, a person designated by the trust, or certain nonprofit charitable organizations, upon reasonable request, to inspect the animal, the premises where the animal is maintained, or the books and records of the trust. The bill would accept these trusts from the application of specified provisions generally regarding the termination of trusts.

The people of the State of California do enact as follows:

SECTION 1.
§15212.

(a) Subject to the requirements of this section, a trust for the care of an animal is a trust for a lawful non-charitable purpose. Unless expressly provided in the trust, the trust terminates when no animal living on the date of the settlor's death remains alive. The governing instrument of the animal trust shall be liberally construed to bring the trust within this section, to presume against the merely precatory or honorary nature of the disposition, and to carry out the general intent of the settlor. Extrinsic evidence is admissible in determining the settlor's intent.

(b) A trust for the care of an animal is subject to the following requirements:

   (1) Except as expressly provided otherwise in the trust instrument, the principal or income shall not be converted to the use of the trustee or to any use other than for the benefit of the animal.

   (2) Upon termination of the trust, the trustee shall distribute the unexpended trust property in the following order:

   (A) As directed in the trust instrument.

   (B) If the trust was created in a non-residuary clause in the settlor's will or in a codicil to the settlor's will, under the residuary clause in the settlor's will.

   (C) If the application of subparagraph (A) or (B) does not result in distribution of unexpended trust property, to the settlor's heirs under Section §21114.

   (3) For the purposes of Section §21110, the residuary clause described in subparagraph (B) of paragraph (2) shall be treated as creating a future interest under the terms of a trust.

(c) The intended use of the principal or income may be enforced by a person designated for that purpose in the trust instrument or, if none is designated, by a person appointed by a court. In addition to a person identified in subdivision (a) of Section §17200, any person interested in the welfare of the animal or any nonprofit charitable organization that has as its principal activity the care of animals may petition the court regarding the trust as provided in Chapter 3 (commencing with Section §17200) of Part 5.

(d) If a trustee is not designated or no designated or successor trustee is willing or able to serve, a court shall name a trustee. A court may order the transfer of the trust property to a court-appointed trustee, if it is required to ensure that the intended use is carried out and if a successor trustee is not designated in the trust instrument or if no designated successor trustee agrees to serve or is able to serve. A court may also make all other orders and determinations, as it shall deem advisable to carry out the intent of the settlor and the purpose of this section.

(e) The accountings required by Section §16062 shall be provided to the beneficiaries who would be entitled to distribution if the animal were then deceased and to any nonprofit charitable corporation that has as its principal activity the care of animals and that has requested these accountings in writing. However, if the value of the assets in the trust does not exceed forty thousand dollars ($40,000), no filing, report, registration, periodic accounting, separate maintenance of funds, appointment, or fee is required by reason of the existence of the fiduciary relationship of the trustee, unless ordered by the court or required by the trust instrument.

(f) Any beneficiary, any person designated by the trust instrument or the court to enforce the trust, or any nonprofit charitable corporation that has as its principal activity the care of animals may, upon reasonable request, inspect the animal, the premises where the animal is maintained, or the books and records of the trust.

(g) A trust governed by this section is not subject to termination pursuant to subdivision (b) of Section §15408.

(h) Section §15211 does not apply to a trust governed by this section.

For purposes of this section, "animal" means a domestic or pet animal for the benefit of which a trust has been established.

IV. Sample *"Pet Protection Trust"* for *"Sparky"* the Dog

SAMPLE: *PET PROTECTION TRUST* for SPARKY

(Place a Photo of Your Pet Here)

Pet Estate Plan & *Pet Protection Trust* for

"SPARKY"

Pet Protection Trust **ESTABLISHED IN ACCORDANCE WITH CALIFORNIA PROBATE SECTION §15212**

THIS Revocable Trust Agreement and Declaration of Trust (this "Agreement") is made on _____ by and between JANE DOE, a resident of Santa Clara County, State of California, hereinafter called the "Trustor," and JANE DOE, in this Agreement called the "Trustee." The Trust created by this Agreement shall be called the "JANE DOE *Pet Protection Trust.*"

Section 1 GRANT OF PROPERTY

The Trustor declares that she is holding the property set forth on Schedule A as Trustee under the terms and conditions of this Trust Agreement. The Trustor further declares that the property subject to the terms of this Agreement, the income there from and the proceeds thereof is her separate property and shall remain her separate property after its transfer to this Trust. Other property acceptable to the Trustee may be added to this Trust by the Trustor or any other person by means of any Will, Codicil, proceeds of life insurance policies, lifetime transfers, or otherwise. Trustor declares that she is establishing this trust for the Protection of her pet toy fox terrier, *Sparky*, pursuant to Section §15212 of the California Probate Code and that is her intent that this trust be construed and interpreted so that it is a valid trust for the care of her above named animal in accordance with the provisions of Section §15212.

Section 2 IDENTIFICATION
Section 2.1 Family

The Trustor is unmarried. The Trustor has no children either living or deceased. The Trustor has a pet toy fox terrier by the name of *Sparky* who she has owned for approximately five years. This dog has been a loyal, faithful and loving companion to her and it is her wish and desire to establish this trust for the sole care and benefit of this pet during the pet's lifetime. Upon the death of the pet, this trust shall cease and terminate and be distributed as further provided in this trust agreement.

Section 2.2 Identity of Trustees

The Trustor shall be the initial Trustee of the Trust. If the Trustor fails or ceases to act as Trustee, then such person or persons as she may designate by written instrument shall act as successor Trustee. The Trustor may at any time designate a co-trustee to serve at with her, or a successor Trustee to serve in her place. If the Trustor ceases or fails to act as Trustee and no such written designation have been made, then *Maria Flores* shall become Trustee. If he fails or ceases to act as Trustee, then such person or persons as she may designate by written instrument shall act as successor Trustee. No bond shall be required of any Trustee acting hereunder, whether or not nominated or appointed by name in this Agreement.

Section 3 PROVISIONS APPLICABLE DURING THE LIFETIME OF THE TRUSTOR

This Section applies while the Trustor is living, and thereafter shall have no further force or effect.

Section 3.1 Use of Net Income and Principal

While the Trustor is living, the Trustee shall pay to or apply for the benefit of *Sparky* such amounts of the net income and principal as the Trustee deems advisable and for the health, education, maintenance, or support of the dog *Sparky*. Any net income not distributed shall be accumulated and added to principal.

true

Section 3.2 Revocation and Amendment
SECTION 3.2.1

At any time or from time to time, this Trust may be revoked, in whole or in part, by the Trustor. This power of revocation shall be exercised by written notice delivered by the Trustor to the Trustee. In the event of such revocation, property in the Trust subject to such revocation shall revert to the Trustor as the Trustor's separate property.

SECTION 3.2.2

This Trust may be amended, in whole or in part, by the Trustor at any time. This power of amendment shall be exercised by written instrument delivered by the Trustor to the Trustee. Any amendment changing the duties, powers, or responsibilities of the Trustee shall require the Trustee's consent. The Trustor's powers to revoke and amend this Trust Agreement are personal to the Trustor and shall not be exercisable on Trustor's behalf by any other person, except that revocation or amendment may be made on behalf of the Trustor by an attorney-in-fact acting on behalf of the Trustor under a then effective durable or other power of attorney granted by the Trustor expressly authorizing the attorney-in-fact to amend a trust created by the Trustor, or may be authorized by court order.

After the death of the Trustor, this Agreement may not be revoked or amended.

DISPOSITION OF RESIDUARY TRUST ESTATE UPON THE DEATH OF THE TRUSTOR

Section 4.1 DISTRIBUTIONS FOR THE CARE OF THE PET

So long as *the pet dog, Sparky*, is living the Trustee shall provide for the *benefit of Sparky* as much of the net income and principal of the trust as the Trustee, in his or her absolute discretion, determines for the care, support and maintenance of *Sparky*. Any undistributed income shall be accumulated and added to principal. The Trustee is directed and authorized to provide for the care and maintenance of *Sparky* in accord with the standard of care and maintenance that I have provided *Sparky* over the years I have owned him. Without limiting the generality of the forgoing charge, it is intended that such expenses would include: food, regular veterinary care and professional grooming, insurance, pet sitting and temporary boarding fees, professional training, exercise and recreational costs. In addition, the Agent is to provide *Sparky* with any and all dietary supplements or medicine proscribed or recommended by *Sparky's* any licensed veterinary physician attending to him. In addition, if *Sparky* shall suffer from a medical or physical condition or illness and the Trustee determines, based on a written opinion of a veterinary professional who has personally examined *Sparky*, that it would be more humane to euthanize *Sparky*, then the Trustee is authorized to do so at the cost and expense of the this Trust.

The Trustee, in the Trustee's sole and absolute discretion may, without prior court approval, terminate any trust established hereunder if the Trustee determines that the fair market value of the principal of a trust has become so low in relation to the cost of administration that continuation of the trust will defeat or substantially impair the accomplishment of its purposes. This Trust will terminate upon the death of *Sparky*. Upon termination of the Trust, the remaining trust property shall be distributed to the *Santa Clara County Humane Society.*

Section 5 NO PAYMENT OF DEATH TAXES AND EXPENSES

Section 5.1 Death Taxes

This Trust shall not bear any portion of any gift, inheritance tax, estate or other death tax incurred by reason of the Trustor's death. In addition, This Trust shall not bear any portion of any expenses of administration incurred in administering my estate or any other trust, which the Trustor has either established, or is a beneficiary of at the time of her death.

Section 6 DUTIES AND POWERS OF THE TRUSTEE

Except as otherwise expressly provided in this Agreement, the provisions of this Section shall apply to and govern each Trust under this Agreement. In addition, to the powers given a Trustee in this Agreement, a Trustee shall have all of the powers conferred on Trustees generally under California law.

Section 6.1 General Duties of Trustee

The Trustee shall hold, manage, invest, and deal with the Trust in whatever form the same may take and however the same may be invested from time to time, collect all income of the Trust, pay all costs, taxes, and other expenses incidental to the Trust and dispose of the net income and principal of the Trust in all respects as directed by the provisions of this Agreement.

Section 6.2 Action by Trustees

During such time as two or more persons are acting as Co-Trustees, any action taken by a majority of the Co-Trustees shall be binding, and third parties may rely on such action. The nonconsenting Co-Trustees shall not be liable for the actions of the majority. During such times as two or more persons are acting as Co-Trustees, some or all of the powers of a Co-Trustee may be transferred to one or more of the other Co-Trustees by execution of a written instrument signed by all the then-acting Co-Trustees.

Section 6.3 Trustee's Powers

In addition to the powers, authority, and discretion conferred upon the Trustee by the provisions of this Agreement or by law, the Trustee is authorized to do the following:

1) To retain as an investment for the Trust and in the same form as received by the Trustee all or any of the property received by the Trustee, and the Trustee is under no obligation or duty to diversify the investments of the Trust;

2) To accept additions to the Trust from any and every source;

3) To manage, invest, and reinvest the Trust property and each and every part thereof, with power to purchase or otherwise acquire every kind of investment, real, personal, or mixed, specifically including, but not limited to, improved

and unimproved real property, corporate and government (whether local, state, or federal) obligations of every kind, stocks (both preferred and common), shares of mutual funds of any and every character, and stocks, obligations, and shares or units of common trust funds of any corporate fiduciary; and also physical commodities, futures, contracts, and options;

4) To sell, convey, grant options, exchange, lease without limit as to term, borrow and hypothecate, or encumber Trust property by mortgage, deed of trust, pledge, or otherwise, maintain and operate margin accounts, borrow on margin, partition, divide, improve and repair, and to do and perform any and all other acts and things deemed by the Trustee necessary or advisable in the management, investment, and reinvestment of the Trust that may be done by an absolute owner of property, including any such transactions between or among separate trusts hereunder; and to purchase or otherwise acquire and maintain unproductive property, including life insurance policies, and to exercise all rights of ownership granted on such policies;

5) To hold real or personal property of the Trust in the name of a nominee or nominees, with or without indicating the Trust character of said property, the Trustee being responsible for the acts of such nominee or nominees with respect to any property so held;

6) To employ attorneys, custodians, investment counsel, accountants, bookkeepers, or other persons to render services for the Trustee or in the Trustee's behalf with respect to all matters pertaining to the Trust and to pay

from Trust funds the reasonable fees and compensation of such persons for their services, said fees and compensation to be paid in addition to fees paid to the Trustee;

7) To determine in connection with the distribution of Trust assets the timing of each distribution, the assets to be allocated to each share of the Trust, and whether assets of the Trust should be distributed pro rata or non-pro rata among the persons or trusts entitled to the various shares of the Trust, including the discretion to allocate community property of the Trustors on a non-pro rata basis, such determinations to be made with or without regard to the cost basis of each such asset, as the Trustee shall decide; the Trustee may satisfy any pecuniary gift wholly or partly by distribution of property other than money; and the Trustee may make, or not make, in the Trustee's discretion, reimbursement to any beneficiary or adjustment in any beneficiary's interest, shares, or distribution by reason of such actions, as the Trustee shall deem appropriate;

8) To commence or defend, at the expense of the Trust, such litigation with respect to the Trust or any property of the Trust estate as the Trustee may deem advisable, and to compromise or otherwise adjust any claims or litigation against or in favor of the Trust, both during the term of the Trust and after the distribution of Trust assets, provided that the Trustee shall have no obligation or duty with respect to any litigation or claims occurring after distribution of Trust assets unless the Trustee is adequately indemnified by the distributees for any loss in connection with such matters;

9) To carry insurance of such types and in such amounts as the Trustee deems advisable, at the expense of the Trust, to protect the Trust estate and the Trustee personally against any hazard;

10) To abandon any property or interest in property belonging to the Trust when, in the Trustee's discretion, such abandonment is in the best interest of the Trust and its beneficiaries;

11) To have all the rights, powers, and privileges of an owner with respect to any securities held in Trust, including, but not limited to, the powers to vote, give proxies, and pay assessments; to participate in voting trusts, pooling agreements, foreclosures, reorganizations, consolidations, mergers, and liquidations, and incident to such participation to deposit securities with and transfer title to any protective or other committee on such terms as the Trustee may deem advisable; and to exercise or sell stock subscription or conversion rights.

All decisions of the Trustee concerning the exercise or non-exercise of the powers described in this paragraph are within the Trustee's discretion.

Except as otherwise provided by law, the Trustee shall not be liable to any person interested in the Trust for any act or omission of the Trustee.

Section 6.4 Records and Accountings

In accordance with Section §15212 of the *California Probate Code*, each year the Trustee shall provide the beneficiary or beneficiaries who are to receive the remaining trust property upon the termination of this Trust with an accounting. The contents of this accounting are set forth below.

1. *Contents of Account.* At such time as any trust established hereunder becomes irrevocable, the Trustee shall each year thereafter provide the *Humane Society of Santa Clara County* with a written accounting, in the following form and substance:

   (a) The accounting shall include a statement of receipts and disbursements of principal and income that have occurred during the last complete fiscal year of the trust or since the last account.

   (b) A statement of the assets and liabilities of the trust as of the end of the last complete fiscal year of the trust or as of the end of the period covered by the account;

   (c) A statement of the Trustee's compensation for the last complete fiscal year of the trust or since the last account, and the basis upon which the compensation was determined.

   (d) The Trustee shall have the sole and absolute discretion to value, in good faith, the trust assets at their fair market value for reporting and accounting purposes. The Trustee may, but is not required, to obtain at the expense of the trust, professional appraisals or valuations of any trust asset.

2. *Exclusive Duty to Account.* The Trustee's duty to account and report to the beneficiary is governed exclusively by the terms and provisions of this Section. The Trustee shall not be required to provide any beneficiary with any data, information, report or accounting which would otherwise be required under the *California Probate Code.* Except as otherwise provided herein, any decision to provide a beneficiary with an accounting, report or other information shall be at the Trustee's sole and absolute discretion. However, upon termination of a trust established under this Agreement, the Trustee shall provide each of the beneficiaries of the terminating trust with an accounting, the contents of which shall be as provided in this Section.

3. *Objections to Accounting by Beneficiary.* If the recipient of an accounting fails to object to the Trustee's accounting by providing written notice of the objection to the Trustee within 180 days after receiving a copy of the accounting, the beneficiary shall be barred from asserting any claim against the Trustee regarding an item that is adequately disclosed in the account or report. An item is adequately disclosed if the disclosure meets the requirements of paragraph (1) of subdivision (a) of Section §16460 of the *California Probate Code.* After the expiration of the 180 period, the accounting shall be final and conclusive as to such beneficiary as if settled by a court of competent jurisdiction, for transactions disclosed in the accounting as provided above.

4. *Settlement of Account.* After settlement of the account by agreement of the parties objecting to it or by expiration of the 180 day period, the Trustee shall no longer be liable to any beneficiary of the Trust, including unborn, unascertained, and

contingent beneficiaries, for transactions disclosed in such account, except for the Trustee's intentional wrongdoing or fraud.

5. *Suspension of Duties.* The duties of the Trustee to maintain records and provide accountings as set forth herein shall be suspended for the period when a Trustor is acting as a Trustee for the Trust.

Section 6.5 Compensation of Trustee

Each Trustee shall be entitled to reasonable compensation for services as a Trustee, and such compensation shall be charged against the income or principal of the Trust in such manner and proportions as the Trustee shall deem proper and fair to all persons interested in the Trust.

Section 6.6 Exculpation and Indemnification of Trustee

No individual acting as Trustee of a Trust established under this Agreement shall be liable to any beneficiary for the Trustee's acts or failure to act, except (1) for breach of trust committed intentionally, with gross negligence, and bad faith or with reckless indifference to the interest of the beneficiary, or (2) for any profit that the Trustee derives from a breach of trust. An individual acting as a Trustee shall be protected and held harmless from any and all liability and cost (including attorneys' fees) in taking or defending any actions on behalf of a trust established under this Agreement. Further, a Trustee acting hereunder shall have the right to be indemnified or reimbursed for any expense or cost incurred by the Trustee in the course of administering this Trust.

Section 6.7 Resignation and Removal of Trustee

Any Trustee hereunder may resign at any time, without stating or giving any reason for his, her, or its resignation, by giving written notice to the Trustor, or if the Trustor is deceased then to the residuary beneficiary or beneficiaries named to receive the trust property upon the termination of the Trust. The Trustor may remove a Trustee at any time. After the death of the Trustor, a Trustee may only be removed for cause by a court of competent jurisdiction. Upon resignation or removal of the Trustee, the vacancy shall be filled pursuant to the foregoing provisions of this Agreement.

Section 6.8 Successor Trustee Not Liable for Acts of Predecessors

No successor individual or corporate Trustee shall be liable for, or be under any duty to see to the propriety of, the acts or omissions of the Trustee or Trustees occurring prior to his, her, or its taking office as such Successor Trustee.

Section 7 ADMINISTRATIVE PROVISIONS

Section 7.1 Written Notice of Events

Until the Trustee shall receive written notice of any death or other event upon which the right to payments from any trust hereunder may depend, the Trustee shall incur no liability for disbursements made in good faith to persons whose interests may have been affected by such event.

Section 7.2 Disclaimers

Any Beneficiary under this Agreement may disclaim all or any portion of any property or interest in property given to such Beneficiary pursuant to the terms of this Agreement, such disclaimer to be made pursuant to *Probate Code* sections 260 et seq. or *Internal Revenue Code* section 2518.

Section 7.3 Payments To or For Benefit of Beneficiaries

The Trustee is authorized to make payments under this Agreement either to the Beneficiary entitled to such payment or to the conservator of the Beneficiary's person or estate or to such other person or persons as the Trustee may deem proper to be used for the benefit of the Beneficiary.

Section 7.4 Singular Includes the Plural

Except where the context otherwise requires, the singular includes the plural when referring to executors, trustees, guardians, conservators, or custodians.

Section 7.5 Code References

All references in this Agreement to the *"Probate Code"* are to the *Probate Code of the State of California,* as amended from time to time. All references in this Agreement to the *"Internal Revenue Code"* are to the *United States Internal Revenue Code of 1986,* as amended from time to time.

Section 7.6 Applicable Law

The validity of this Trust and the construction of its beneficial provisions shall be governed by the laws of the State of California in force from time to time, and shall be construed in accordance with *California Trust Law*, including Division 9 of the *California Probate Code*. California law shall apply regardless of any change of residence of the Trustee or any beneficiary, or the appointment or substitution of a Trustee residing or doing business in another state.

Section 7.7 Jurisdiction and Venue

Any dispute or litigation arising with respect to the Trust or the Trust Agreement shall be decided by a court with jurisdiction over the Trust or other appropriate forum for the resolution of dispute as agreed upon by the parties involved.

Section 7.8 Severability Clause

Should any of the provisions of this Agreement be for any reason invalid, the invalidity thereof shall not affect any of the other provisions of this Agreement, and all invalid provisions hereof shall be wholly disregarded.

IN WITNESS WHEREOF, the parties hereto have executed this Agreement this _____ day of _____, 20_____.

Signature _____
JANE DOE, PET Owner (Trustor)

Signature _____
JANE DOE, PET Owner (Trustee)

Witness _____
NAME (Witness)

Signature _____
Notary of the Public

V. Template *"Pet Protection Trust"* for Your "Companion Pet"

(Place a Photo of Your Pet Here)

Pet Estate Plan & *Pet Protection Trust* **for**

"Pet Name _____"

Date: _____

Pet Owner's Name: _____
Pet Caregiver/Guardian's Name: _____
Pet Financial Caregiver/Trustee's Name: _____

The _____*Pet Protection Trust*

THIS Revocable Trust Agreement and Declaration of Trust (this "Agreement") is made on _____, by and between _____ a resident of _____ County, State of _____, hereinafter called the "Trustor," and _____ in this Agreement called the "Trustee."

The Trust created by this Agreement shall be called the "_____" *"Pet Protection Trust."*

GRANT OF PROPERTY AND DESIGNATION OF PET

The Trustor declares that the Trustor is holding the property set forth on Schedule A as Trustee under the terms and conditions of this Trust Agreement ("Trust").

The Trustor further declares that the property subject to the terms of this Trust, the income therefrom and the proceeds thereof is the Trustor's separate property and shall remain the Trustor's separate property after its transfer to this Trust.

Other property acceptable to the Trustee may be added to this Trust by the Trustor or any other person by means of any Will, Codicil, proceeds of life insurance policies, lifetime transfers, or otherwise.

Trustor declares that the Trustor is establishing this trust for the Protection of the Trustor's animal designated and described on Schedule B of this Trust, and that this Trust is a trust established pursuant to Section §15212 of the *California Probate Code "Probate Code")* for the protection and care of the animal designated and described on Schedule B.

It is Trustor's intent that this Trust be construed and interpreted so that it is a valid trust for the care of the animal designated and described on Schedule B in accordance with the provisions of §15212 of the *Probate Code.*

Term of the Trust

This Trust shall commence on the date of this Trust document and shall continue until revoked or terminated by the Trustor as provided below or the lifetime of the pet animal designated on Schedule B. This Trust shall become irrevocable upon the death of the Trustor and shall continue thereafter until the death of the pet animal designated and described on Schedule B of the Trust. Upon the death of the pet animal designated on Schedule B, this trust shall cease and terminate and shall be distributed as further provided in this trust agreement.

Identity of Trustees

The Trustor shall be the initial Trustee of the Trust. If the Trustor fails or ceases to act as Trustee, then such person or persons as she may designate by written instrument shall act as successor Trustee. The Trustor may at any time designate a co-trustee to serve at with her, or a successor Trustee to serve in her place. If the Trustor ceases or fails to act as Trustee and no such written designation has been made, then _____ shall become Trustee. If _____ fails or ceases to act as Trustee, then such person or persons as _____ may designate by written instrument shall act as a successor Trustee. No bond shall be required of any Trustee acting hereunder, whether or not nominated by name or appointed pursuant to the terms of this Trust or by a Court order.

PROVISIONS APPLICABLE DURING THE LIFETIME OF THE TRUSTOR

This Section applies while the Trustor is living, and after the death of the Trustor shall have no further force or effect.

Use of Net Income and Principal

While the Trustor is living, the Trustee shall pay to or apply for the benefit of the animal designated and described on Schedule B such amounts of the net income and principal as the Trustee in the Trustee's sole and absolute discretion deems advisable or necessary for the health, education, maintenance, or support of the animal designated and described on Schedule B. Any net income not distributed shall be accumulated and added to principal.

Revocation and Amendment

At any time during the lifetime of the Trustor, this Trust may be revoked or terminated, in whole or in part, by the Trustor. This power of revocation and termination shall be exercised by written notice delivered by the Trustor to the Trustee. In the event of such revocation or termination, property in the Trust subject to such revocation or termination shall revert to the Trustor as the Trustor's separate property.

In the event, the Trustor becomes incompetent or incapacitated so as not be able to act as Trustee hereunder, the Trustee acting during such incompetency or incapacity shall have full power and authority to pay or apply for the benefit of the animal designated and described on Schedule B such amounts of the net income and principal as the Trustee in the Trustee's sole and absolute discretion deems advisable or necessary for the health, education, maintenance, or support of the animal designated and described on Schedule B. Any net income not distributed shall be accumulated and added to principal. For purposes of this provision, a Trustor shall be deemed to be incompetent or incapacitated if the Trustor declares in writing that the Trustor is suffering from a physical or mental condition which has rendered the Trustor incompetent or incapacitated or two licensed medical physicians have declared in writing that the Trustor is suffering from a physical or mental condition which has rendered the Trustor incompetent or incapacitated.

This Trust may be amended, in whole or in part, by the Trustor at any time. This power of amendment shall be exercised by written instrument delivered by the Trustor to the Trustee. Any amendment changing the duties, powers, or responsibilities of the Trustee shall require the Trustee's consent.

The Trustor's powers to revoke, terminate and amend this Trust Agreement are personal to the Trustor and shall not be exercisable on Trustor's behalf by any other person. After the death of the Trustor, this Agreement may not be revoked or amended. Further, this Trust shall not be terminated except in accordance with the terms of this Trust or as otherwise authorized under _____ (state) law.

DISPOSITION OF RESIDUARY TRUST ESTATE UPON THE DEATH OF THE TRUSTOR

DISTRIBUTIONS FOR THE CARE OF THE PET

After the death of the Trustor and so long as the pet animal designated and described on Schedule B of this Trust, is living the Trustee shall pay to or apply for the benefit of the animal designated and described on Schedule B such amounts of the net income and principal as the Trustee in the Trustee's sole and absolute discretion deems advisable or necessary for the health, education, maintenance, or support of the animal designated and described on Schedule B.

Any undistributed income shall be accumulated and added to principal. The Trustee is directed and authorized to provide for the care and maintenance of the pet animal describe on Schedule B of this Trust in accord with the standard of care and maintenance that the Trustor has provided to the animal during the Trustor's lifetime. Without limiting the generality of the forgoing charge, it is intended that such expenses would include: food, regular veterinary care and professional grooming, insurance, pet sitting and temporary boarding fees, professional training, exercise and recreational costs. In addition, the Trustee is authorized and directed to provide the animal with any and all dietary supplements or medicine proscribed or recommended by any licensed veterinary physician attending to the animal.

In addition, if the animal designated and described on Schedule B is suffering from a medical or physical condition or illness and the Trustee determines, based on a written opinion of a veterinary professional who has personally examined the animal, that it would be more humane to euthanize the animal, then the Trustee is authorized to do so at the cost and expense of the this Trust.

The Trustee, in the Trustee's sole and absolute discretion may, without prior court approval, terminate any trust established hereunder if the Trustee determines that the fair market value of the principal of a trust has become so low in relation to the cost of administration that continuation of the trust will defeat or substantially impair the accomplishment of its purposes. This Trust will terminate upon the death of the animal designated and described on Schedule B of this Trust. Upon termination of the Trust, the remaining trust property shall be distributed to _____.

NO PAYMENT OF DEATH TAXES AND EXPENSES
Death Taxes

This Trust shall not bear any portion of any gift, inheritance tax, estate tax or other death tax incurred by reason of the Trustor's death. In addition, This Trust shall not bear any portion of any expenses of administration incurred in administering the Trustor's estate or any other trust which the Trustor has established during the Trustor's lifetime or in the Trustor's will or by reason of the exercise of a power of appointment held by the Trustor or any trust in which the Trustor is a beneficiary of at the time of the Trustor's death.

DUTIES AND POWERS OF THE TRUSTEE

Except as otherwise expressly provided in this Agreement, the provisions of this Section shall apply to and govern the Trust established under this Agreement. In addition, to the powers given a Trustee in this Agreement, a Trustee shall have all of the powers conferred on Trustees under _____ (state) law.

General Duties of Trustee

The Trustee shall hold, manage, invest, and deal with the Trust in whatever form the same may take and however the same may be invested from time to time, collect all income of the Trust, pay all costs, taxes, and other expenses incidental to the Trust and dispose of the net income and principal of the Trust in all respects as directed by the provisions of this Agreement.

Action by Trustees

During such time as two or more persons are acting as Co-Trustees, any action taken by a majority of the Co-Trustees shall be binding, and third parties may rely on such action. The nonconsenting Co-Trustees shall not be liable for the actions of the majority. During such times as two or more persons are acting as Co-Trustees, some or all of the powers of a Co-Trustee may be transferred and delegated to one or more of the other Co-Trustees by execution of a written instrument signed by all the then-acting Co-Trustees.

Trustee's Powers

In addition to the powers, authority, and discretion conferred upon the Trustee by the provisions of this Agreement or by California law, the Trustee is authorized to do the following:

1) To establish on behalf of the Trust bank or other accounts with any financial institution;

2) To retain as an investment for the Trust and in the same form as received by the Trustee all or any of the property received by the Trustee, and the Trustee is under no obligation or duty to diversify the investments of the Trust;

3) To accept additions to the Trust from any and every source;

4) To manage, invest, and reinvest the Trust property and each and every part thereof, with power to purchase or otherwise acquire every kind of investment, real, personal, or mixed, specifically including, but not limited to, improved and unimproved real property, corporate and government (whether local, state, or federal) obligations of every kind, stocks (both preferred and common), shares of mutual funds of any and every character, and stocks, obligations, and shares or units of common trust funds of any corporate fiduciary; and also physical commodities, futures, contracts, and options;

5) To sell, convey, grant options, exchange, lease without limit as to term, borrow and hypothecate, or encumber Trust property by mortgage, deed of trust, pledge, or otherwise, maintain and operate margin accounts, borrow on margin,

partition, divide, improve and repair, and to do and perform any and all other acts and things deemed by the Trustee necessary or advisable in the management, investment, and reinvestment of the Trust that may be done by an absolute owner of property, including any such transactions between or among separate trusts hereunder; and to purchase or otherwise acquire and maintain unproductive property, including life insurance policies, and to exercise all rights of ownership granted on such policies;

6) To hold real or personal property of the Trust in the name of a nominee or nominees, with or without indicating the Trust character of said property, the Trustee being responsible for the acts of such nominee or nominees with respect to any property so held;

7) To employ attorneys, custodians, investment counsel, accountants, bookkeepers, or other persons to render services for the Trustee or in the Trustee's behalf with respect to all matters pertaining to the Trust and to pay from Trust funds the reasonable fees and compensation of such persons for their services, said fees and compensation to be paid in addition to fees paid to the Trustee;

8) To determine in connection with the distribution of Trust assets the timing of each distribution, the assets to be allocated to each share of the Trust, and whether assets of the Trust should be distributed pro rata or non-pro rata among the persons or trusts entitled to the various shares of the Trust, including the discretion to allocate assets of the trust among beneficiaries on a non-pro rata basis, such determinations to be made with or without regard to the

cost basis of each such asset, as the Trustee shall decide; the Trustee may satisfy any pecuniary gift wholly or partly by distribution of property other than money; and the Trustee may make, or not make, in the Trustee's discretion, reimbursement to any beneficiary or adjustment in any beneficiary's interest, shares, or distribution by reason of such actions, as the Trustee shall deem appropriate;

9) To commence or defend, at the expense of the Trust, such litigation with respect to the Trust or any property of the Trust estate as the Trustee may deem advisable, and to compromise or otherwise adjust any claims or litigation against or in favor of the Trust, both during the term of the Trust and after the distribution of Trust assets, provided that the Trustee shall have no obligation or duty with respect to any litigation or claims occurring after distribution of Trust assets unless the Trustee is adequately indemnified by the distributees for any loss in connection with such matters;

10) To carry insurance of such types and in such amounts as the Trustee deems advisable, at the expense of the Trust, to protect the Trust estate and the Trustee personally against any hazard;

11) To abandon any property or interest in property belonging to the Trust when, in the Trustee's discretion, such abandonment is in the best interest of the Trust and its beneficiaries;

12) To have all the rights, powers, and privileges of an owner with respect to any securities held in Trust, including, but not limited to, the powers to vote, give proxies, and pay assessments; to participate in voting trusts, pooling agreements, foreclosures, reorganizations, consolidations,

mergers, and liquidations, and incident to such participation to deposit securities with and transfer title to any protective or other committee on such terms as the Trustee may deem advisable; and to exercise or sell stock subscription or conversion rights.

All decisions of the Trustee concerning the exercise or non-exercise of the powers described in this paragraph are within the Trustee's absolute discretion. Except as otherwise provided by law, the Trustee shall not be liable to any person interested in the Trust for any act or omission of the Trustee.

Records and Accountings

In accordance with Section §15212 of the *California Probate Code*, each year the Trustee shall provide the beneficiary or beneficiaries who are to receive the remaining trust property upon the termination of this Trust with an accounting. The contents of this accounting are set forth below.

1. **Contents of Account.** At such time as any trust established hereunder becomes irrevocable, the Trustee shall each year thereafter provide the beneficiary or beneficiaries who are to receive the remaining trust property with a written accounting, in the following form and substance:

    (a) The accounting shall include a statement of receipts and disbursements of principal and income that have occurred during the last complete fiscal year of the trust or since the last account;

(b) A statement of the assets and liabilities of the trust as of the end of the last complete fiscal year of the trust or as of the end of the period covered by the account;

(c) A statement of the Trustee's compensation for the last complete fiscal year of the trust or since the last account, and the basis upon which the compensation was determined.

(d) The Trustee shall have the sole and absolute discretion to value, in good faith, the trust assets at their fair market value for reporting and accounting purposes. The Trustee may, but is not required, to obtain at the expense of the trust, professional appraisals or valuations of any trust asset.

2. **Exclusive Duty to Account.** The Trustee's duty to account and report to the beneficiary is governed exclusively by the terms and provisions of this Section. The Trustee shall not be required to provide any beneficiary with any other data, information, report or accounting.

3. **Objections to Accounting by Beneficiary.** If the recipient of an accounting fails to object to the Trustee's accounting by providing written notice of the objection to the Trustee within 180 days after receiving a copy of the accounting, the beneficiary shall be barred from asserting any claim against the Trustee regarding an item that is adequately disclosed in the account or report. An item is adequately disclosed if the disclosure meets the requirements of paragraph (1) of subdivision (a) of Section §16460 of the *California Probate Code*. After the expiration of the 180 period, the accounting shall be final and conclusive as to such beneficiary as if settled by a court of competent jurisdiction, for transactions disclosed in the accounting as provided above.

4. **Settlement of Account.** After settlement of the account by agreement of the parties objecting to it or by expiration of the 180 day period, the Trustee shall no longer be liable to any beneficiary of the Trust, including unborn, unascertained, and contingent beneficiaries, for transactions disclosed in such account, except for the Trustee's intentional wrongdoing or fraud.

5. **Suspension of Duties.** The duties of the Trustee to maintain records and provide accountings as set forth herein shall be suspended for the period when a Trustor is acting as a Trustee for the Trust.

Compensation of Trustee

Each Trustee shall be entitled to reasonable compensation for services as a Trustee, and such compensation shall be charged against the income or principal of the Trust in such manner and proportions as the Trustee shall deem proper and fair to all persons interested in the Trust.

Exculpation and Indemnification of Trustee

No individual acting as Trustee of a Trust established under this Agreement shall be liable to any beneficiary for the Trustee's acts or failure to act, except (1) for breach of trust committed intentionally, with gross negligence, and bad faith or with reckless indifference to the interest of the beneficiary, or (2) for any profit that the Trustee derives from a breach of trust. An individual acting as a Trustee shall be protected and held harmless from any and all liability and cost (including attorneys' fees) in taking or defending any actions on behalf of a trust established under this Agreement. Further, a Trustee acting hereunder shall have the right to be indemnified or reimbursed for any expense or cost incurred by the Trustee in the course of administering this Trust.

Resignation and Removal of Trustee

Any Trustee hereunder may resign at any time, without stating or giving any reason for his, her, or its resignation, by giving written notice to the Trustor, or if the Trustor is deceased then to the residuary beneficiary or beneficiaries named to receive the trust property upon the termination of the Trust. The Trustor may remove a Trustee at any time. After the death of the Trustor, a Trustee may only be removed for cause by a court of competent jurisdiction. Upon resignation or removal of the Trustee, the vacancy shall be filled pursuant to the foregoing provisions of this Agreement.

Successor Trustee Not Liable for Acts of Predecessors

No successor individual or corporate Trustee shall be liable for, or be under any duty to see to the propriety of, the acts or omissions of the Trustee or Trustees occurring prior to his, her, or its taking office as such Successor Trustee.

ADMINISTRATIVE PROVISIONS
Written Notice of Events

Until the Trustee shall receive written notice of any death or other event upon which the right to payments from any trust hereunder may depend, the Trustee shall incur no liability for disbursements made in good faith to persons whose interests may have been affected by such event.

Disclaimers

Any Beneficiary under this Agreement may disclaim all or any portion of any property or interest in property given to such Beneficiary pursuant to the terms of this Agreement, such disclaimer to be made pursuant to *Probate Code* sections 260 et seq. or *Internal Revenue Code* section 2518.

Payments To or For Benefit of Beneficiaries

The Trustee is authorized to make payments under this Agreement either to the Beneficiary entitled to such payment or to the conservator of the Beneficiary's person or estate or to such other person or persons as the Trustee may deem proper to be used for the benefit of the Beneficiary.

Singular Includes the Plural

Except where the context otherwise requires, the singular includes the plural when referring to executors, trustees, guardians, conservators, or custodians.

Code References

All references in this Agreement to the *"Probate Code"* are to the *Probate Code of the State of California*, as amended from time to time. All references in this Agreement to the *"Internal Revenue Code"* are to the *United States Internal Revenue Code of 1986*, as amended from time to time.

Applicable Law

The validity of this Trust and the construction of its beneficial provisions shall be governed by the laws of the State of California in force from time to time, and shall be construed in accordance with *California Trust Law*, including Division 9 of the *California Probate Code*. California law shall apply regardless of any change of residence of the Trustee or any beneficiary, or the appointment or substitution of a Trustee residing or doing business in another state.

Jurisdiction and Venue

Any dispute or litigation arising with respect to the Trust or the Trust Agreement shall be decided by a court with jurisdiction over the Trust or other appropriate forum for the resolution of dispute as agreed upon by the parties involved.

Severability Clause

Should any of the provisions of this Agreement be for any reason invalid, the invalidity thereof shall not affect any of the other provisions of this Agreement, and all invalid provisions hereof shall be wholly disregarded.

IN WITNESS WHEREOF, the Trustor and the Trustee of this Trust hereby signs and executes this Agreement this _____ day of _____, 20_____.

Signature _____
FULL NAME, Pet Owner (Trustor)

Signature _____

FULL NAME, PET Owner (Trustee)

Witness _____

NAME (Witness)

Signature _____

Notary of the Public

CERTIFICATE OF ACKNOWLEDGMENT

STATE OF _____ STATE) ss

COUNTY OF _____ COUNTY) ss

On _____, before me, _____ Notary Public, personally appeared _____, who proved to me on the basis of satisfactory evidence to be the person whose name is subscribed to the within instrument and acknowledged to me that he/she executed the same in his/her authorized capacity, and that by his/her signature on the instrument the person or the entity upon behalf of which the person acted, executed the instrument.

I certify under PENALTY OF PERJURY under the laws of the State of _____ (State) that the foregoing paragraph is true and correct. WITNESS my hand and official seal.

NOTARY PUBLIC STATE OF CALIFORNIA

Signature _____

Notary of the Public

Schedule A
Property Subject to this Trust

Schedule B

Designation and Description of Pet Animal
Copy of *"Pet Protection Daily Care Guide*™ *"*

VI. How to Locate a Notary of the Public and Get Your *"Pet Protection Trust"* Document Properly Notarized

Congratulations! As the *"Pet Owner"* you have now finished the two documents (the *"Pet Protection Daily Care Guide*™*"* and the *"Pet Protection Trust"*) to have a complete *"Pet Protection Legal Care Plan"* for your companion pet. The final step involves locating a *Notary of the Public* to ensure that all the correct information has been recorded with the court.

To find a *Notary of the Public*, start by checking with your local bank and/or credit union. Many banks offer free notary services to their customers. Of course, you will need to meet with the notary during the bank/credit union's normal hours, when a notary is on duty. If your bank/credit union doesn't have a notary, or if you aren't near one of its branches when you need something notarized, try a *UPS* Store, *FedEx* Office, a check cashing service, or another location that offers business services.

Before your appointment with the notary, gather the *"Pet Protection Daily Care Guide*™*"* and the *"Pet Protection Trust"* (*"Pet Protection Legal Care Plan"*) document that you have completed. It is important to remember not to sign any of these papers before bringing them to the notary to review with you. The notary needs to witness your signature. The notary will also require proof of your identity *(e.g. a driver's license, passport or other government-issued photo ID will do)*. Notaries must also verify that you understand the documents you are signing. They may ask a few questions to ensure that you do, and also verify that you are not signing the documents against your will.

Your notary will then produce a special journal for the *"Pet Owners"* signature. States do have varying laws, but most require notaries to maintain thorough records. Finally, when asked by the notary, sign and date your *"Pet Protection Trust"* documents. He or she will then affix their seal or stamp to the documents and sign it.

VII. How to Complete Your *"Pet Protection Trust"* and the *"Pet Protection Daily Care Guide*™*"* Online

The *"Pet Protection Legal Care Plan"* book includes all of the information that you need to complete your *"Pet Protection Daily Care Guide*™*"* and the *"Pet Protection Trust"* templates. However, you may find it more convenient to access these templates online rather than using this book to document your choices. To purchase an immediate download of the *"Pet Protection Daily Care Guide*™*"* and the *"Pet Protection Trust"* blank document/templates, you will need to visit our website at *www.PetProtectionLegalCarePlan.com*. The downloadable document is for your own personal use. The authors recommend completing one set of *Pet Protection Trust* documents for each pet in your household. You are given a one-time, non-transferable, "personal use" license to the downloadable *"Pet Protection Daily Care Guide*™*"* and the *"Pet Protection Trust"* (*"Pet Protection Legal Care Plan"*) template.

About the Authors

"Thousands of years ago, cats were worshipped as gods.
Cats have never forgotten this." ~*Anonymous*

Mary G. Anderson, *Author*

Mary G. Anderson is an author, speaker and organizational consultant/coach who is dedicated to helping others define their legacy and live true to it. Through her consulting firm, *Life Management Consulting Group*, she offers products and services to support clients to both start and finish the important projects in their lives. Mary is an advocate of planning ahead to protect yourself, your family, your pets and your business—*just in case*. She also provides coaching support to those who are coping with difficult life altering forever change, transition and loss.

- Founder, *Life Management Consulting Group*
- Author of the *"Pet Protection Legal Care Plan™"* and *"My Estate Management Guide"*
- Former Corporate Training Manager, *Hewlett Packard*, 25 years of experience as an Executive Trainer
- Certified *Conflict Resolution/Mediator Specialist*
- *Fortune 500* Consultant/Management Training Specialist
- Legacy Planning, Business Succession & End-of-Life Planning Products & Customized Training Services

Francis Burton Doyle, Esq., *Co-Author*

Attorney and founder of *WealthPLAN*, Frank Doyle brings nearly 35 years of legal experience in tax, estate planning, probate, trust administration and litigation. *WealthPLAN* offers premier legal expertise in the highly complex arena of significant wealth preservation and transfer. Frank is certified by the *State Bar of California* as a specialist in both Taxation Law and Probate, Estate Planning and Trust Law. Mr. Doyle is a Professor of Law at *Lincoln Law School of San Jose* and an instructor for *Advanced Legal Training Institute, National Business Institute (NBI)* and *Lorman Educational Seminars*.

www.PetProtectionLegalCarePlan.com

Ernam rerios most, officias inulluptat audit quo volo earios incti aborest, sim re soluptatur magnima gnatem quiam niatus, core sitas sapitia temolorem dolore rem inum dolendis quibus ipis re coribus quam hitatendita del maxima volorum iunti conseque quamendit alignis eatiisc ipiendit, venimin ullenda nientin tistis del iliqui te volo magnat aut aut expere pe re res utem quid quo comnis porerchit a sima sit rest, sitam ditat.

Cest adianda ndipsanim liatinis eum volupti arci inctat quatata tatempost elicto modigentur, to iure, volori acerchilis dendit, occullo ribust, et mi, verum eicilit aturiatem illut omnihit paritatis acitas et quo tem ipsant quodict uribus exerchitate vid que poriatis am, quam voluptam vent aut quaspel enimodis sa volore magniam eribusciat ea quam renditatem fugit aut quo et, qui sint ommodis eiur as rem aut eum et reiunt, corum, aditis non rest quis plabo. Ut odita sit, occus modigenihit vent plabore mporum simagnat volor sit quodit quid estis nus molo esto experibus aut laborep udipit ad ut andandam aut earchit eos eveles consero et occullacias esed quam sed earibeaque lit essequam ipsandi officiuribus sitatis volupta tectur res por sint fugia denis simi, quam raerrorro eumqui con restiis inci dis re consequi tem. Andemodis accus moluptat.

Aliciumque omnimus. Igent latet et discias sequost isinulparum unt distrunt perum quam res sus nis sim aute inveligenes rem que vendit dolendit oditatias dolum fugiam harumquibus que odis adia sequis antum, si dipsus eatur, sedis ut rae quam alibus que vel ere rem que omnisse receatum, quiati ne nossit, enit laut laut velitiis diciunt essum hicae nam renis eum aut aliam eost quam sitistiur?

Ebit magnam, tem que moluptatur, tem. Cullorerunt es adigniendit, in porecum quiaerovit elia dolore mi, qui quiatiis ducias et ut alia nem ut rem volupta sundel ium latur?

Ebit vel etur, necae prate nis dolupta cus idus num, sit maximagnist, con natiand ucienis ratius ariam sum ipsuntur autem aceratempor sum lat quatur aspidest hicab il imporese voloratis re volorit asimi, nonsedionsed quo officiis quam autem. Nemporendi cus a conseque laboreped mo et doluptat.

Edit, veliqui omnient qui tem qui rest, que quuntius et quam nihilit estrum, omnihic aercipsam eos est, iuste volorec teceaqu iatius ma volent, earum am hilic tet amus quis mint as sitame prae repudis aut rem aspitatem. Nem atem. Itatem fugit quatiam dias ut odipiti orporrovitas eritat lantium quo od et faccull orporum fuga. Namus es nos sequas eum vero eaque magnitate aut as im derum idit odit repta eum fugit, cuptat incit ipis disciaest liti nes expliam rerspercimus dolores ex et moluptaerro con rae simolorepel incta vitatur autatem ut dolorep erferro enihilla nobitendae con pliquibus excercipitat in cus.

Bissunt. Is atiusam aut quatiis alibus vitat.

What people are saying about the
"Pet Protection Legal Care Plan" book:

"This well-written, informative, and compassionate book should be read be every pet-owner. Many of the books that are currently available regarding end-of-life planning for pets are either filled with legal jargon or very complicated to understand. I just wanted a simple roadmap to get all the information lined up for the care of my dog, *Buttercup*, in the event of my death. The *"Pet Protection Legal Care Plan"* is so easy-to-use and simple—it can be completed in one afternoon. I know now that my dog is protected after I'm gone." ~ *Barbara, Dog Owner, Palm Springs, CA*

"This is the guide I have been looking for to make sure my little kitty named *"Suey"* has a plan for her care, just in case. Since I am elderly and live alone, the thought of something happening to me and not knowing if she would be rescued and/or cared for immediately, is upsetting to me. Now I have a plan in place so my neighbor Delores will care for *"Suey"*. Luckily I have my *"Pet Protection Daily Care Guide™"* completed so that my neighbor has all the details regarding the location of our veterinarian and my cat's finicky meal schedule. I have peace-of-mind now." ~*Noreen, Cat Owner, Seattle, WA*

"I often have to travel for my job and I have dog walkers, overnight pet sitters, etc. to help me out with the care of my two Golden Retrievers, *Ellen* and *Barney*. I know when I head out-of-town that each caregiver has a copy of the *"Pet Protection Daily Care Guide™"* so the caregivers know the pet's daily schedule for meals, exercise, play and sleep times. Everyone who has a pet should read this book, each chapter is designed to make sure that no matter what happens the pet will be protected. I am able to handle my business and work challenges while knowing that my pets are happy, content and waiting with wagging tails for my return!" ~*John, Dog Owner, Gilroy, CA*

"My hunting dog is named *Chester*. He has been through extensive training and he is my steady companion on our ranch. I have already completed an estate plan to protect my wife and children so I was pleased to find out that I could complete some simple documents to protect *Chester*. The *"Pet Protection Legal Care Plan"* is as easy as 1-2-3 to finish and once I had all the details in order about my dog, I called up my attorney and dropped a copy by his office to be added to my other estate planning documents. It feels good to know that I have put my thoughts into writing and now there is a plan in place for my family and *Chester*." ~*Robert, Dog Owner, Death Valley, CA*

"Because my kitty, *Jenny*, is deaf—I have had to make certain provisions to make her life more comfortable. She is also partially blind too and must be kept inside the house at all times. I was happy to complete the *"Pet Protection Legal Care Plan"* so I know now that no matter what might happen to me, my little princess will always be taken care of properly. There is so much helpful, important and new information here. Without reading this book, I would have never guessed how important and easy it is to prepare a solid pet protection plan. As pet owners we need to get the legal documentation done and to get a signed commitment from the caregiver to protect our pet. Completing this process has given me the confidence of knowing *Jenny* will always be protected. ~*Barbara, Cat Owner, Truckee, CA*

"This book, the *"Pet Protection Legal Care Plan"*, provides a step-by-step procedure to protect your pet if you should become disabled or deceased. The online *"Pet Protection Trust"* template is a user-friendly instructional guide that explains clearly what to do, when to do it and how to do it! I am glad that a diligent, responsible lover of dogs (the author) worked closely with an Estates and Trusts attorney (the co-author)—to get every detail covered. I would recommend this book to anyone who is seeking the peace-of-mind that comes from knowing their final wishes are legally protected and will be honored." ~*Jim, Dog Owner, Redding, CA*

Made in United States
Orlando, FL
03 April 2022

16442684R00088